SISTERS

Essays by Carol Saline

Photographs by Sharon J. Wohlmuth

RUNNING PRESS

Philadelphia ○ London

20 19 18 17 16 15

Digit on the right indicates the number of this printing.

Library of Congress Cataloging-in-Publication Number 93–87592

ISBN 1–56138–450–X

Cover design by Toby Schmidt

Jacket and interior photographs by Sharon J. Wohlmuth

Interior design by Ken Newbaker

Edited by Melissa Stein

Typography: Centaur MT by Richard Conklin

Printed in China by Lee-Fung Asco Printers Ltd

This book may be ordered by mail from the publisher. Please add $2.50 for postage and handling. *But try your bookstore first!*

Running Press Book Publishers

125 South Twenty-second Street

Philadelphia, Pennsylvania 19103–4399

To my sister, Beth, with my enduring love and admiration for your courage and dedication as a seeker of truth.

And, Gary, I love you.

—S. J. W.

To my sister, Patsy, with gratitude and love for who she is and what she has meant to my life.

—C. S.

Contents

Acknowledgments

My thanks to Eliot Kaplan, editor of *Philadelphia Magazine,* for giving me the
time and the support to write this book; Erin Arvedlund and Melissa Birnbaum for their
research assistance; Nzinga for her make-up services; Helen Flaherty for her prompt tape
transcriptions; Tim Haas for his patience and help with my lack of computer skills;
Helene Singer for juggling so many last-minute changes in our travel schedule;
my agent, Ellen Levine, for her belief in this project and her encouragement to pursue it.
And to my close friends and family for their interest and their nurturance.

—C. S.

I wish to thank a wonderful circle of family and friends whose spirit and support
navigated me through the making of this book: Judith Harold Steinhauser, Linda Herskowitz,
Toby Schmidt, Marcia Goldner, Gerry Benene, Marilyn Shapiro, Akira Suwa, Gary Haynes,
Clem Murray, Nancy Steele, Stuart Teacher, and Lawrence Teacher.

—S. J. W.

My sister has always had the knack of giving me terrific birthday presents I'd never think of buying for myself. But, by far, the best gift I ever got from her was an original framed needlepoint that she'd commissioned someone to stitch. The workmanship was beautiful, but it was the inscription that made my mascara run. In just a few words it summed up the eternal essence of our relationship. It simply said: *A sister is a forever friend.*

When I hung my present on the wall, it occurred to me that this would be a wonderful theme for a book. So I was in the right mindset when my friend, photographer Sharon J. Wohlmuth, told me she'd long been thinking about doing a photographic project on sisters.

We were chatting about books and ideas one hot summer afternoon when Sharon commented, "Because of my relationship with my sister, Beth, I've always been intrigued by the spirit of sisters. I can't tell you how often I've watched two women walking down a street and intuitively, I know they're sisters. There's a certain intimacy that makes them so different from close friends. Sisterhood is such a powerful relationship."

By the end of our conversation, we'd agreed to collaborate on this book.

Of the many relationships in a woman's life, the bond between sisters is unique, stretching and bending through periods of closeness and distance, but almost never breaking. Sisterly ties tend to have fewer emotional knots than the ones that bind mothers and daughters. Sisters are girlfriends, rivals, listening posts, shopping buddies, confidantes, and so much more.

Some sisters never move beyond childhood rivalry. Most, however, develop an affectionate attachment that becomes a critical support system in their middle and later years. Margaret Mead said, "Sisters are probably the most competitive relationship within the family, but once sisters are grown, it becomes the strongest." Her sister commented, "You can tell your sister to go to hell in twelve different languages and if you need a quarter, she'll lend you a quarter."

Research shows that older women who have strong connections with their sisters are less likely to be depressed. In one study, women said they felt the world was a safer place because they had sisters to depend upon in times of crisis. My experience interviewing the women in this book repeatedly confirmed this. Sisters function as safety nets in a chaotic world simply by being there for each other.

Brothers share the biological link, but they're . . . well . . . just different. They rarely seem as emotionally glued as girls who grew up under the same roof. What sets sisters apart from brothers—and also from friends—is a very intimate meshing of heart, soul, and the mystical cords of memory.

There are physical memories: washing in the bathtub, giving good-night kisses and snuggles, watching each other's bodies grow and change; scrutinizing who got bigger breasts and slimmer hips, who menstruated first, which one can eat anything and never gain an ounce, who's aging better, who has more wrinkles. . . . There are social memories: boyfriends, battles over clothes, shopping sprees, school plays, ballet lessons, family outings. And, of course, there are priceless emotional memories: heartfelt advice, unquestioned loyalty, late-night phone marathons; contemplating who was Daddy's little girl, who was Mom's favorite, who got the most attention, who felt rejected.

The interweaving of these funny, joyful, angry, painful, and historic memories creates the foundation—solid or shaky—on which every sister-relationship rests.

Among the sisters we met, those with the warmest, closest sentiments shared several characteristics. Their parents were committed to assuring that their daughters would be friends. Loving sisters exhibited a high regard and respect for each other. In their hearts they felt like equals regardless of where they lived, if they had daily, weekly, or monthly contact, whether there were great differences in income, lifestyle, or achievement. When one sister was in need, the other became caretaker or care giver. Knowing that a sister could be relied upon in a crisis—or simply to share wonderful news—was a great comfort: "I couldn't wait to tell my sister" is a phrase we heard over and over.

At the end of my interviews, I'd often ask sisters to talk about what they meant to each other. There was usually a moving exchange that had all of us reaching for a tissue. Then they'd say with the awe of having received a precious gift, "Oh, I never realized you felt that way!" Clearly, this special something sisters have is neither taken lightly nor taken for granted.

Most sisters want what they perceive as an ideal relationship; what most sisters have is a relationship occasionally flawed by conflict. We chose in this book to focus on sisters who genuinely like each other, but we also wanted to include a few who do not get along. They, too, expressed common feelings, particularly a sense of loss. With sadness and some embarrassment, they talked about what the world thinks a sister should be and how they wished their relationship reflected that model.

While affection is the natural bonding agent between sisters, in its absence, anger may substitute as an equally powerful adhesive. Feuding sisters—even those who no longer speak—maintain a psychic connection through their rage. The space between them isn't empty at all; it roils with feeling. "Being hated by my sister feels like a curse," is how one put it. Many women were eager to privately discuss with me the pain of their alienation, but unwilling to appear in a book where they'd be identified. A few even asked me to call their estranged sister and mediate a meeting. I attempted it a few times, but it never worked—one would be willing; the other coldly resistant.

In contrast to the balanced relationship of loving sisters, angry sisters typically complained about feeling exploited or depleted. One had too much of something—money, parental approval, vanity, ego—while the other felt cheated or resentful. It wasn't material possessions that separated them nearly as much as emotional baggage. As one women told me, "Nobody can be closer than a sister, but nobody can hurt you more."

Photographing and writing about sisters confirmed for Sharon and me something we've always known, but perhaps not fully appreciated: how lucky we are to have sisters we dearly love.

"My vision, when I started this project, was to capture the shared intimacy of the biological and emotional bonding of sisters," says Sharon. "Through my photographs I wanted to reflect the unique mystery that is sisterhood. Sometimes that required patiently waiting for a moment when the connection would reveal itself. More often than not, despite the many distractions and restrictions that can characterize a photo shoot, there did emerge a settled moment when the spark I was looking for ignited. While each of the women I photographed had her own individual story, there was similarity to all the relationships. They were all sisters and their sisterhood was magic."

For Sharon and me, creating *Sisters* has been an exhilarating experience. We want to thank all the wonderful women we met who took two strangers into their hearts and so openly shared some of their deepest thoughts. Our lives have been enriched by becoming, if only for a short time, a part of theirs.

We created this book as a gift to our own sisters, but we dedicate it as well to all those women blessed with sisters who have made the highs in life more meaningful and the lows more bearable. We hope you will treasure these stories and images as much as we do.

Anna Margaret and
Hannah Marie: The Klales Sisters

Once upon a time there was a six-year-old girl named Anna who looked just like a pre-Raphaelite principessa. Anna lived with her parents in a big house near the woods, and although she was happy drawing and coloring by herself, sometimes she was just a tiny bit lonely for a playmate. Then, one day, her mother had wonderful news. She was going to have a baby! "Well, it had better be a sister," said Anna. "If it's a boy, we'll give it away."

That night, alone in her room, she tried to imagine what it would be like to have a sister. She knew exactly what she wanted for the baby's name: Hannah. She'd chosen it because she could already spell it by adding an "H" to the beginning and end of her own name.

"Well, let's see," Anna said to herself as she lay in the dark. "As soon as Hannah comes home, I'll hold her and feed her and give her a bottle. Later on I'll teach her how to walk, and when she gets a little older, I'll give her my tricycle. And we'll play games like hide-and-seek, and I'll show her how to be good in school.

"We won't be just friends. We'll be sisters. Alike. Only one of us will be bigger than the other. Sometimes we'll fight but I'll give her one of my dollies and that's how we'll make up. We'll tell each other secrets, and Hannah will love me as big as the world."

Anna snuggled down in her canopy bed, her curls spread over the pillow, and fell asleep, dreaming about how she and Hannah would live happily ever after.

Several months later, Anna nestled alongside her mother, gingerly cradling her tiny, pink, hour-old sister in her arms.

"Am I dreaming, Momma?" she whispered. "See how her eyes are closed. She must be tired. I think we should keep her. She's too cute to give away."

Suddenly, Hannah began to cry. Anna, her little heart filled with the joy of having her very own baby sister, wept, too. And so began their lifelong journey of sharing each other's happiness and comforting each other's tears.

Eli and Liz:
The Martinez
Sisters

As little girls, Eli and Liz liked nothing better than to make pretty bouquets from the flowers from their grandmother's garden. As big girls, nothing has changed: they work side by side every day at their elegant flower shop in Miami's hip South Beach. "We've just always been together," says one or the other—it's hard to tell which, because they look, think, and speak so much alike. "It's just like one life," says Eli. (Or is it Liz?)

Both agree there are no feelings left unexpressed between them. "If we get mad at each other, it lasts two minutes and we forget the whole thing," Liz says. Yet once, when Liz had a potentially life-threatening accident, what both feared most was that something they needed to say had been left unspoken.

"It was not long ago," Eli says, "very early in the morning. Liz had fallen in the tub and hurt a gland in her groin. She was in terrible pain. Mom called me right away and said, 'You've got to come *now*.' I told my husband that Liz was hurt, threw on some clothes and ran the block to their condo. Liz was pale, really pale. Her groin was swollen up, all black and blue. I convinced her she must go to the hospital, and I rode in the ambulance. I remember they were playing a Rod Stewart song, "Some Guys Have All the Luck," and I thought that this song would always remind me of Elizabeth in pain.

"They had to operate right away. I remember telling the anesthesiologist, 'This is my one and only sister. Please, please take special care of her.' As they wheeled her away on the stretcher, she was so weak she could barely wave. Suddenly I realized, 'Oh my God. I didn't get to talk to her. I didn't say *I love you*.' "

Liz cuts in. "I was lying there thinking the exact same thing. That here I might die and I didn't get to say good-bye to my sister. I wanted to tell her how much she meant to me. I thought of all the great moments we'd had together and all the things I should have said. So I want to tell her now, 'You're the best thing in my life.' "

"You, too," Eli says, smiling. "You, too. You, too."

Coretta and Edythe: The Scott Sisters

My dear sister Coretta,
I am sitting here tonight thinking about us. How close we were as children, sharing everything, doing everything together, always the leaders, always picked for the plays and the concerts because we were talented and attractive. The kind of kids teachers just knew would cooperate. When I went to Antioch before you, I learned about sibling rivalry in one of my courses, and I didn't believe there could be such a thing. We certainly never competed or were jealous—even if you did have more boyfriends. And you've forgiven me for telling you there was no Santa Claus.

Do you remember when you were five, already so physically strong, and you helped me pull the first bucket of water from the well outside of our house? That became a metaphor for our lives. All these years we've pulled each other up, supported each other, and taken care of each other. Even Martin saw that. He called us the twins. He'd be giving a speech in some big auditorium and he'd say, "My wife isn't here tonight. But her sister is in the audience—so if I want to see Coretta, I just look down there at Edythe."

I've never told you this, but Martin comes back to me in my dreams. It's always when we're up against the wall and you don't know what to do. He comes to me smiling and joking and says it's going to be all right. That's when I call you and get very positive and tell you we'll find a way. Sometimes I think we would have been even closer if Martin hadn't died. You were my best friend for so long, but now there are always so many others around you, wanting a piece of you, there isn't always as much room for the two of us.

When we were growing up you always told people you thought I was the smarter one, that I knew everything. But I have learned from you. You've taught me to live each day as fully as I can, because no one knows what tomorrow will bring. You taught me to rely on the spiritual force in the universe, how not to worry or to be afraid. And I hope I've made you laugh and brought some joy into your very serious life.

I was trying to explain to someone what keeps our relationship working and I used that phrase from *The Prophet* by Kahlil Gibran: I said, "We have spaces in our togetherness." Doesn't that describe us well? We've never been the kind to say things; we just do for each other. So, for once, I wanted to tell you how blessed I feel to have a sister that I'm comfortable with and that I like as well as love.

Edythe

Dear Edythe,

Your beautiful letter carried me back to those days when it was more common for us to pick up a pen than a telephone. I particularly remembered a letter you'd written to me when I was in Boston studying music at the New England Conservatory. I hadn't told you that Martin had proposed to me on our first date, several months earlier. Because this was the most important decision I could make in terms of my future, I wanted to make it myself, without your influence. I prayed and struggled and then I had a revelation in a dream. I saw Daddy King, Martin's father, smiling at me approvingly. The next morning I woke up with a sense of inner peace that I interpreted to mean the relationship would work out. Right after that, your letter came, as if you'd read my mind. "Don't be silly, girl," you wrote. "You know how difficult it is to find intelligent, stable, well-adjusted men"—a whole string of adjectives. And then you wrote, "You won't have your career as you dreamed it, but you will have your career."

That summer you came to live with me in Boston and we used to play games with Martin on the phone because he couldn't tell us apart. And remember how he wanted to test me on my cooking? You and I prepared this fine dinner for him. We really were old-fashioned girls who knew how to cook. Afterwards he'd tell people, "I asked Coretta to cook a meal for me and she dispatched Edythe. The two of them teamed up on me!"

You've always known instinctively just how to make me comfortable and support me. I will never forget the day after Martin's funeral, when you packed up your son and came to stay with me. The fact that I never had to ask meant so much to me. You just knew ahead of time how deeply I was going to need you and you were there. I will always be grateful for your foresight and your presence. Having you, my sister, in the house for two years with me and as a surrogate mother to my children, especially when I had to be away so often, was a comfort no one else could have provided. And when there were little frictions among my staff, you were always careful to keep negative things away from me so that I wouldn't worry.

I'm so glad you've been with me whenever anything important has happened, although I still regret that you were ill and couldn't come to Oslo for the Nobel Peace Prize. But I have wonderful memories of all the times you traveled with me on special occasions, giving advice and helping me write letters and speeches. Writing was never my forte, but you had that talent back in high school when you were editor of the paper. I always admired that you had such a good mind and a grasp of things. You did so much reading and thinking. I was more an activist kind of child. It seemed to me you always had so much information—you had that way of eavesdropping on the adults—and I loved when you'd tell me things and share the secrets you'd found out.

If you hadn't gone to Antioch College first and made a place for me and pulled me in, I'd have missed having the experience that prepared me for my role today. The emphasis on multiculturalism and the democratic community there were the perfect training for my life's work.

I wish that your teaching commitments at Cheyney State and my busy schedule would allow us to visit more often. When you're around I laugh more, and I need that because I tend to be so serious-minded. You have a way of finding humor in anything. You can pull the theater out of life. Being with you, I can be completely myself. You appreciate the stresses I have being a public figure, meeting people's expectations, fulfilling a role. When it's just us, I can be myself and know you'll love and understand me no matter what. You don't want anything from me except my happiness.

I'm very lucky. I don't have a husband, but I do have a sister. A sister I can talk to about personal things I wouldn't tell anyone else. A sister who does things for me, consoles me, comforts me. A sister with whom I can share my burdens and my joys. It's very hard in this world to find someone who can walk in your shoes, but you come closer to that than anybody. A lot of sisters are not friends. You, Edythe, like Maya Angelou has said, are my sister-friend.

Coretta

Anna, Jane, and Kate: The McGarrigle Sisters

Jane was expected to be the brilliant musician: she was a church organist at 14, and also excelled in school.

Anna would be the socialite, flitting about at lovely parties where the ladies wore gloves and hats, sipped champagne, and ate strawberries.

Kate was slated to become the engineer.

Those were the roles Frank McGarrigle chose for his three daughters—but it didn't turn out quite the way he planned. Had he lived to see Kate and Anna become internationally-known folk singers, though, he might have taken some of the credit. After all, wasn't he the one who had them harmonizing around the 1883 Steinway in the living room as soon as they could carry a tune? Didn't he encourage them to play any old broken-down instrument that fell into his hands—a banjo, an accordion, a guitar, a zither? Music was the air these sisters breathed, their fun and their entertainment through the long cold winters in a tiny, isolated mountain town outside Montreal. And the first one to get to the piano didn't get stuck in the kitchen doing dishes.

"We had this ridiculous background growing up as bohemian Anglos in a French village. Everybody else ate dinner promptly at six; we ate whenever the food was ready. Our parents never wanted us to be ordinary," Kate says with great affection. "Maybe because there were no boys, we were taught we could do anything we wanted without limits. They designed

us to be well-versed in many things, to be good thinkers and to be close friends."

As they huddle around the wooden kitchen table of the cozy house where they grew up—and where they still return on weekends to visit their 90-year-old mother—it's quite obvious the McGarrigles are more than just sisters and business partners.

"When we're not around each other, we have these other roles," Anna says. "We're this one's mother or that one's wife. But when the three of us get together, wherever it is, we immediately revert back to being the sisters we were growing up: Jane's the oldest; Kate's the youngest; I'm forever in the middle."

"I've had the feeling from different men I've been with," Jane says, "that no matter how devoted or loyal I am to them, they think my sisters have a kind of priority. They sense that we are more important to each other than to anyone else."

"Anna's husband thinks we're interchangeable," says Kate. "That any coupling of the two of us is equally as good as any other coupling of the other two. In fact, we really do have different things with each other. When Jane and I are driving on a trip, we love to talk business and money. When Anna and I are together, we're having fun and doing music or she's reading Jack Kerouac to me or we're planning to stop somewhere to buy stupid dresses or books on art and architecture. The nicest part of all for me is when I come to Anna or she comes to me and says, 'I've written a song. Do you want to help me work it out musically?' And for hours we just sit there and try things."

"All three of us have this incredible physical closeness," Anna says. "When Kate and I are on the road we never have our own rooms, although we could. We always share. It's like a marriage without sex."

"I know what she likes and what she doesn't," Kate says, "She doesn't have to tell me when I'm pushing or pulling too hard. For instance, Anna is much more reasonable and grounded than I am. I wanted to go further in our careers than she did. Go on the road more. Follow the formula for success. I saw the possibilities for us and tried to drag her along. But some people won't be dragged. At one point Anna asked me, 'Do you want to do it by yourself?' But I wouldn't, because it isn't fun without her company. For us, working together is like going on a vacation or being in summer camp. It's not the same alone."

"Wherever we go in the world, we filter our experiences through a similar lens," Jane explains. "We will collapse with laughter at something nobody else finds funny. We always seem to get a big kick out of the same things. It's impossible to keep our business and our lives from running altogether. When I first started managing my sisters, I tried very hard to be structured, to schedule meetings and such. But then I'd call Kate to discuss a problem and she'd be making gazpacho and we'd wind up trading recipes. There's this thing that flows through whatever we do, whether it's visiting, cooking, working, shopping."

"Actually Anna buys a lot of things for me because she knows I hate to shop," Kate says.

"But, Kate," Anna demurs, "you're the one who might all of a sudden send us a hydrangea or decide to buy everybody underwear."

"I think," Kate replies, "that we're just always in each other's minds."

And certainly in each other's hearts. When Kate was going through a messy divorce, Anna wrote a song for her:

> No scheme and no direction
> with only one way to turn.
> Pack up all your children,
> come home to our love and concern.
> Kitty, come home.

"We've sat around this kitchen table for 45 years echoing the message of that song," Jane says.

"Yeah," Kate replies. "My guess is we'll last longer than our careers."

"The career thing is just a blip," Anna says. "Maybe our songs will go on. Maybe not. But this sister thing we have will go on as long as we live."

Maria and Michele: The D'Ambrosio Sisters

Michele and Maria are each other's favorite people. They have never fought for longer than three hours. They exchange extravagant gifts, wear each other's clothes, vacation together, and jabber on the phone at least ten times daily—and that's in addition to the three days a week they work side by side in Michele's gourmet food business. Orphans since their teens, both insist that raising each other for the last twenty years has made them inseparable.

Maria says, "When people tell me, 'What a shame you don't have parents,' I always say, 'But I have this incredible sister, Michele, who nurtures all my needs and fulfills me.' I don't even mind that she worries about me all the time. It's just so nice to know somebody cares."

Michele echoes those sentiments. "I survived the death of our parents, but I can't imagine surviving without my sister. I wouldn't want to be alive without her."

Without Maria, Michele would have no one to validate her history. "Everything I know, from as far back as I go, she knows, too. When I see a chocolate donut, I can say to Maria, 'Remember how Daddy loved chocolate donuts?' and she knows exactly what I'm feeling."

Their closeness defines not only the meaning of family, but also the meaning of friendship. "My sister is the friend who shows me what I want from other friends," says Michele. "She sets the standard everybody else has to match."

For Maria, Michele simply outweighs any other priority.

"I was once involved with a Frenchman, and I'd gone to Monaco for six weeks. Michele took a vacation in Spain with the man she lives with and drove twelve straight hours to visit me. The minute she arrived I realized I was more excited to see her than to stay with this guy in France. It wasn't an easy choice. Philadelphia can't compare to the beaches of Mónaco. But marrying him meant I'd have to live far away from my sister. So I left."

Erin, Kelly, and Christy: The Turlington Sisters

"People ask us what it's like to have a famous sister," Kelly says, talking about Christy, the supermodel. "We just don't notice any difference. When she comes home to visit, she still cleans out our closets, tells us what to wear, gives us expensive clothes she's worn only once or twice. She's the most generous person you could imagine. Takes us on vacations to Aspen, Jamaica. When we visit her in New York, she makes us a part of her crowd."

Erin could not agree more. "The three of us are still best friends. If there were anyone in the world I could spend time with, do anything with, it would be my sisters. We have qualities that balance each other. Like Christy is so open and friendly and Kelly is cute and smart."

"And you have good judgment about people and you're very funny and silly," says Kelly.

For Christy, her sisters represent a constant in the whirlwind, demanding world of international modeling. "They are my best friends," she says, echoing Kelly. "The people I talk to most often. The people who make me feel most comfortable. I'm with different groups of people all the time, which means I don't have a chance to get all that close and, to tell the truth, I'm not sure I want to.

"Even growing up, I started and stopped relationships a lot. We lived in Danville, California, then Miami for four years, then back to Danville, then I went to New York. Only my sisters have been with me the whole time. We've shared everything. Without using words, we just *know* things about each other. There's a security in that."

These three girls, born roughly a year apart, were raised more like triplets. Whenever one developed an interest in something, their parents saw to it that the others got involved. That meant everybody camped out in the backyard, went hunting with their dad, took piano and ballet lessons, rode horses, and played soccer and softball.

"Oh, they bickered sometimes," their mother remembers. "But they always made excuses for the other, stood up for each other. Their personalities were different, but they had a real appreciation for each other's assets. You could just see the bond. It was always them against us."

They were so much The Three Musketeers that once, in a fit of teenage rebellion, they even ran away from home together. Of course, being good girls at heart, they had someone call their parents to report that they were fine and were staying with friends. After two weeks, on Thanksgiving Day no less, they ended their adventure—just in time to be reunited for a turkey dinner.

Even when Christy was chosen over Kelly for a modeling career, there wasn't a ripple of jealousy. The girls had been horseback riding at a stable in Florida when a photographer on a magazine assignment spotted them and asked if they'd like to pose for a photo shoot. Kelly was more at ease in front of the camera, but the agency preferred Christy, because at 14, she'd already reached a model's height of 5'9" while Kelly, at 16, had peaked at 5'6". Kelly, pretty and popular as a prom queen, was much too busy fending off the boys to feel slighted. "I was just happy for my sister's success," she says.

Today, Kelly is living in Los Angeles, married, and is about to make aunts of her sisters. Erin has opened a jazz club and restaurant in San Francisco, made possible in part by Christy's investment. And Christy is soaring all over the globe on assignments. Yet they remain as close as when they were little girls playing with their Barbie dolls.

"My sisters are guaranteed friends for life," Kelly says. "I know it doesn't necessarily have to be that way. But that's how it is with us. We have friends with sisters who don't get along. Like them, we know what buttons to push. But out of respect we don't push them. There's never a reason to hurt your sisters. Never was, never will be."

Lindsey and Eryn: The Elkin Sisters

"Wanna play dress-ups, Lindsey? I'm gonna be the mommy and the movie star."

"Then I wanna be a fairy."

"Okay. You can wear the blue dress because I wore it last time. Those shoes are too high for you. You'll fall down. Look, these are gooder."

"You live in a castle, Eryn, and I live in a fairy house. I'm gonna drive my car to visit you."

"You should fly 'cause you're a fairy. You know, like butterflies with wings. And you're coming to visit me because we're sisters and we haven't been together in a long time and we're sad because we miss each other."

"I'll fly in through a special hole and give you a big hug. It makes me feel nice when I hug you."

"Well, Mommy hugs are a little better. Sister hugs are second."

"That's not fair, Eryn."

"But she's a grown-up; you're a kid. It doesn't mean I don't like your hugs."

"Then I don't like your hugs either."

"Oh, silly. I love your hugs. See. I'm hugging you tight. Now let's have a tea party."

Nancy and Becky: The Young Sisters

Becky Young and Nancy Matheson, identical twins, were born in 1939, ten minutes apart. In their 49th year, Nancy, a heavy smoker, was diagnosed with inoperable lung cancer. Becky immediately put her life as a teacher and photographer on hold to help her sister die. Nancy chose to spend her last days as she'd spent her first, so the twins moved back in with their parents in the little town in western Massachusetts where they'd grown up.

"Toward the end," Becky haltingly recalls, "the cancer got to Nan's brain. She was full of morphine. Really out of it and not making much sense. Yet when I asked her, 'What's your name?' she said, 'Becky-Nanny.' How strange she remembered that. Becky-Nanny was what we used to call ourselves as kids.

"Then, one night, I heard her breathing change over the intercom. Immediately I knew that something was wrong. Our parents had gone to bed and I slipped into her room alone. She'd been sleeping all day, but now her eyes were open with only the whites showing.

"I'd made a pact with Nan that no matter what, she'd depart this world like she came into it, beside me, the way we'd been together in the womb. I crawled in bed with my body up against her, holding my sister in my arms, the closest person in my life. And very softly I began to sing "You Are My Sunshine, My Only Sunshine."

"I'd started singing that song to cheer her up one afternoon in the hospital when she was scared to go for some kind of test. It made her smile, and we harmonized like we'd done when we were kids. After that, our singing became a kind of nightly ritual. I told her that when the time came she didn't harmonize with me, that's how I'd know she was gone.

"For about twenty minutes I sang and sang and counted her breaths. They got less and less, and my Becky-Nanny never sang back."

Aimee and Amanda: The Hector Sisters

When the Hector twins were three years old, one fell off the bed. The other, playing downstairs, suddenly began to cry. When they were eight, Amanda tumbled down the basement stairs, and Aimee, up in the bedroom, felt a sharp pain in her rear end. And once, Aimee injured her knee in a gym class accident and had to be rushed to the hospital. Amanda, completely unaware of her sister's injury, limped around the school all afternoon complaining that her knee hurt.

Twins are truly sisters under the skin, two bodies joined by a common soul. Without each other, the Hector girls actually feel incomplete. Amanda was once invited to a bar mitzvah by a boy in her science class who didn't know Aimee. "I went by myself but it wasn't fun. Something was missing. Being around other people without my sister is hard." When Amanda got sick at summer camp and had to come home, Aimee insisted on leaving with her.

They knocked down a wall in their house so they could share a bedroom. "Sometimes we climb in bed together," Aimee says. "I love Amanda so much. If I'm scared about something, she's right there next to me."

Do they fight like other sisters? Of course. "When we get really mad, we divide our room with a piece of tape. It never stays up more than ten minutes."

"And when we have a fight with a friend, we automatically take each other's side. It makes it hard on our friends, because our loyalties are always first to each other."

Are they ever jealous? "Well, when Aimee did so excellent in soccer and got all those goals, I was kind of jealous she was getting so much attention."

"But Amanda, you're a better singer and more artsy. You get to do the solos in our singing group."

"And how about the time we tried out for the school play, and the teacher said we could share the part. That was so stupid. Everybody else gets their own part and we have to share." The one area where sharing isn't a problem is their modeling career, a profession they've been pursuing since they were toddlers. "If someone doesn't want both of us for a job, we take turns," Aimee says, and Amanda finishes, "They don't know who they're getting anyway."

Do they ever get bored spending so much time together?

"Are you kidding? It's like having a best friend around for your whole life." Still, Amanda admits that every now and then, "It's fun to be home sick and all alone with Mommy." But by lunchtime they can no longer endure being apart, and they must talk on the telephone.

In an effort to make the twins less dependent on each other, their mother enrolled them in different classes when they started school. Recently she persuaded them to stop dressing as twins by promising to buy them individual wardrobes so that, between them, they'd have twice as many clothes.

"We liked to dress alike because it gave us attention and at first, we were afraid that without matching outfits no one would. . . ." Amanda says. ". . . notice us anymore," Aimee continues. "But that didn't happen," they both chime in.

"I had this idea yesterday," Aimee says, "and I couldn't wait to tell my sister."

"But when she started telling me," Amanda picks up, "I already knew what her idea was before she said it."

"Like the time we had that course together," Aimee goes on, "and you would raise your hand to ask a question, and it would be the same question I was ready to ask. It got so, if I saw her hand up, I just lowered mine."

Amanda jumps in. "Sometimes, in a mirror I think I'm seeing Aimee when it's actually me. I remember once we were alone in a hotel, just the two of us in the room. I got up to go to the bathroom and on the back of the door was a mirror that I didn't know was there. When I went by, I thought I saw Aimee's reflection, but that was impossible because she was back on the bed. Then I realized I was really looking at myself. Isn't that weird?"

"I guess it's hard to understand our relationship," Aimee says. "We're attached beyond regular sisters. Once I was Amanda. We were one; now we're two, but we're still part of each other. We're the same, even if our personalities are different. I love her not because she's like me. She *is* me."

They think so much alike that in conversation, their words are practically interchangeable. Ask them what would happen if they both fell in love with same boy? "We'd shoot it out for winners like we do everything else."

How about if one got accepted into a better college than the other? "We'd both go to the same place. We'd never let something like that come between us."

Do they think they'll get married some day? "Yes, but maybe we can have a big house and live in different wings. It's hard to imagine having a relationship with anybody that's closer than ours."

When you're 14-year-old twins who've never spent a night apart, it's even harder to imagine being old and, worse yet, alone. Aimee muses, "I think that when we grow up and get old, if one of us dies, the other one will die pretty soon after that. I hope we're lucky enough to die at the same time."

"Me, too," says Amanda. "I want us to die together."

Joan and Ann:
The Petitt Sisters

Joan and Ann grew up together in different worlds. They ate at the same table under the same roof, had the same five brothers, the same parents—but for nearly forty years, that was about all they thought they had in common.

"I really wasn't aware of her," Ann says. "It was like she grew up in another family. I never knew she wanted a sister, and I never knew I needed a sister."

What Ann might have labeled indifference, her younger sister Joan read as loathing. "I didn't think she liked me at all, and if my own sister didn't like me, I must be defective. That affected me all my life. She made fun of me because I had blonde hair, because I wanted her to play Barbie dolls with me, because I took ballet lessons. I figured these must all be things wrong with me."

"I was jealous of her ballet thing," Ann says. "Joan represented what pretty girls were supposed to be— the favorite, the chosen."

"And I was afraid of Ann. She was too loud, rowdy, and mean, causing fights in the house. Because she scared me, I stayed away from her. I felt maybe if I wasn't in her face, she'd like me better."

There were few healthy attachments in their tempestuous family. Mother was an alcoholic; Father, a compulsive eater and workaholic whose mistress was an open secret.

"I felt like an outsider," Ann says, "attacked by everyone in the family because I *liked* my dad. He was my buddy. I survived by spending a lot of time outside alone hiding out in the grass, watching the bugs and being peaceful. I don't remember doing anything with Joan."

Joan was certain she'd been adopted. "At least that would have explained everything. But I coped by being careful not to make waves, by tap-dancing around everything and jumping to do what people wanted. And what I wanted most was a big sister. I'd watch my girlfriends who had close sisters and think, 'Why can't *I* have that?' Funny thing was that as much as I tried

to stay away from anyone who reminded me of Ann, I kept being drawn to women like her, and I would do everything I could to win them over."

Eventually, Joan's desire to understand her fears and insecurities led her to counseling. "After I worked out my issues around males, there was still this big hole inside me, and I realized I was looking for my sister."

By then, Ann had moved from Cleveland to Charlotte, North Carolina, toting with her the family baggage. "I had to get away so I could work on who I really was and find my identity." Years passed with minimal contact, although Joan wrote now and then and sometimes sent a little present. "I still wanted Ann to like me."

Ann read the letters and thought, "Joan has this nice life, nice husband. She's building a career. I was real proud of her. I knew she'd left school, then gone back, and that was kind of an inspiration to me." But Ann never put her feelings on paper or reached for the phone. And on the rare occasions when she did come home to Cleveland and the sisters saw each other, the old hostilities flared up.

Joan isn't quite sure why, two years ago, she accepted her brother's invitation to drive five hundred miles to visit Ann for the weekend. "I guess I had to slay this dragon. I thought, 'There's got to be something good there I'm missing. My brother thinks she's terrific and she *is* my sister.'"

Ann was thrilled when she heard that Joan and her brother were coming. "I'd figured none of them cared about me. I was just the pain in the ass who'd left home. The only time they ever visited was on the way to Florida. So I was elated and honored they were coming now—just to see me. I felt accepted."

For once, life followed the fairy tale. "We weren't there five minutes," Joan says, "when I realized Ann wasn't the same person. She was warm, wonderful, and loving. We ended up leaving the hotel and camping out at her apartment, like a slumber party, and before long we were saying, 'My God, we're so much alike.' I can look at her and laugh because we have the same hips. I guess most sisters do that, but we never did."

The next day they went hiking in the mountains and gave each other an uninterrupted hour to drop their defenses and swap stories. Ann learned about "the trauma Joan had in her abusive marriage. I had no idea what crap she'd been through and it hurt. I wanted to cry and hold her and comfort her and say how sorry I was that I never knew."

"You *did* say that," Joan reminds her. "And you made it so much better. When you told me that you barely knew I existed as a kid that took a lot of the pain away from me."

Together, they began to unlock their past and build a future. "I'd blocked out so much," Ann says. "Now I have memories and someone to reference things with. Joan is teaching me to see a side of my mother that logic tells me had to exist, but I never saw. We're remembering some of the good, crazy stuff we did as a family. The laughing. Building forts in the living

room. It wasn't all bad. This has helped me to center, to find a part of my life I'd lost. I realize there is a bond here connecting us that you can't have with anyone else but a sister, and that's real good for me. I feel I've walked through a doorway into a new world."

Joan has found that by uniting with Ann, she's improved her other relationships. "I'm no longer trying to suck everybody dry because of what I evidently needed. I don't have to be afraid anymore. Now that I know Ann didn't dislike me, I must not have been so bad after all. I feel I have a real sister now, somebody I can call and say this hurts or feels good and she's not going to make fun of me."

Ann replies, "I always knew I had sisters, but now I have a friend in Joan, and that's more valuable to me." (An older sister, Mimi, remains on the fringe of this reconciliation until, Joan says, "she realizes that healing can take place in a family.")

In the meantime, Ann and Joan are catching up on the childhood they never shared. Recently they met for a weekend in New York. "We were walking down the street," Ann says, "laughing in the rain—two soggy rats, soaking wet. People were staring at us because we were having so much fun." Later, back in their hotel room, they pardoned each other for the past.

"I forgive you, Ann, for the little girl part of me you hurt," Joan whispered.

"I love and accept you just as you are," Ann answered. "I'm so grateful we've rounded the bend."

Aiii . . . ai . . . ai . . . caramba. Presenting to you those Cuban bombshells, the fabulous Scull twins, talking about their lives and their art—which, truth to tell, are hard to distinguish.

They paint much the way they live, side by side, in brilliant technicolor and boundless optimism. Their highly praised folk art—large canvasses full of humor and energy, featuring three-dimensional clay figures—often depicts scenes from the pre-Castro Cuba of their childhood. The recollections of Haydee fill in the gaps left by Sahara, and vice-versa.

"Always, since we are *chiquita*, our art very elaborate. Our minds like cameras, full of ideas. One remember what the other forget."

Now here they come, bouncing into the room, aging Kewpie dolls with scarlet lips, tippy-tapping on their three-inch, spike-heeled sandals, dyed red this very morning to complement the outfits they whipped up on their little sewing machine. Their bedroom doubles as an open closet for the vast wardrobe of costumes they call their clothes—tight-fitting, colorful, scoop-necked dresses that hug their broad, sashaying hips and emphasize their ample bosoms.

Happy, they surely are! Happy to be alive. Happy to be safe in Miami. Happy to be painting what they want, beyond the reach of a dictator. And, most of all, happy to close their eyes each night side by side in their big double bed, jabbering endlessly about their plans for the future and their memories of the past . . . until one of them falls asleep.

"We can never be separate," says Haydee. "She inside me. I inside her. We always inside here, in the heart."

That spiritual thread connected the twins the one and only time that circumstances erected a physical barrier: In 1969, desperate for artistic license, Haydee left Cuba with her two children on a freedom flight. Sahara stayed behind to care for her dying husband and didn't escape until three years later. On the rare occasions they managed to speak on the phone, Haydee would ask Sahara what she ate that day. "If she eat fish, then I eat fish, too. That make me feel close.

"We are very lucky girls. Always very *affinidad*. Never disco dance separate. Life for us is pink. Happy color. And together makes us strong. Four arms. Four legs. One heart. One mind. One soul. Always."

Midge and Dixie:
The Carter Sisters

The day was warm, the air fragrant with the scent of flowers. Four-year-old Midge Helen, and her six-year-old sister, Dixie Virginia, nicknamed Diddie, were planning a major social event. They raided Mother's closet for pretty, colorful scarves, and tied some around their waists, draping others over the peach trees to fancy up the garden. With exquisite care they laid out tiny cups and saucers brought home from the toy department of Daddy's big store in town. Then, with great ceremony, they invited Gina, their mother, and Mama Carter, their grandmother, to join them for tea and lemonade.

Playmates were scarce in McLemoresville, Tennessee (population two hundred), but that barely accounts for why Dixie and Midge are such deliciously dear friends.

"Oh my. I can't remember a time we didn't get along," Dixie says without hesitation. "Mother had a rule that if we fought, no matter who started it, she'd spank us both. We'd go to laborious pains to sneak off for a fight somewhere she wouldn't catch us, and by the time we got to the barn or wherever, we'd lose our steam and forget about it. We even divided the icing when Mama baked a cake. She'd call us in, her little lambs, to lick the pan, and we'd draw a line right down the middle to make sure the other one got enough. Our parents always made a big point of being sure we got equals.

"We slept in the same bed from the time we were born until we moved to town (Huntington, population three thousand) because the school was better. Then we had twin beds in the same room. Our wonderful house in McLemoresville had nothing but fireplaces downstairs to heat it. In the winter, before we went to bed, Mama Carter would come over from her house next door and hold up a blanket in front of the fire. Gina would hold the other blanket up, and they'd tell us stories. When the blankets got hot enough, Midgey and I would scamper up the stairs ahead of them, and they'd wrap us up together, pile more quilts on top, and we'd go to sleep under all this weight, curled up like two little spoons."

Decades later, the sweet spirit of their childhood glows in their adult eyes when they sit down to talk about each other. They cuddle up; their Southern accents thicken; the years melt away and they become as tender as little girls.

"Long after Gina stopped dressing us alike," Dixie continues, "we were allowed to dress as we wanted, and we still chose to dress the same. Miss Eunice, a wonderful seamstress, made all our clothes. We'd be taken in the beginning of the season to the piece goods department in Daddy's store and—would you believe—we'd pick the very same material and patterns, at different times. And—cross my heart this is the truth—at least once a season on different sides of the country we bought our daughters dresses of the exact same fabric. It happened over and over again.

"When we'd gone our separate ways after college, we'd write letters home that would arrive at the same time and say pretty much the same thing. Our children still say that when they were little and we came up behind them, they couldn't tell which one of us it was because our hands felt the same. Isn't that extraordinary?"

"What I find amazing," Midge remarks, "is how Dixie has this very psychic way of reaching out to me emotionally, especially when I'm down. Before my third child was born, she was doing summer stock in North Carolina. Out of the blue, she called home and told Gina, 'I think Midgey needs me.' She flew to California and by the time she got to my house, I'd fallen down the front steps and broken my ankle. It being close to my due date, she just stayed to help. Now, Dixie does not love to do housework, but she cleaned my house from top to bottom and then went off and bought every single thing in the grocery store. Food to cook, a thing to hold paper cups, a new toilet brush. She went nuts."

"But you are the most loving, unselfish sister anyone ever had," Dixie interrupts. "Midge despises crowds," she explains. "Her idea of a huge party is four people. But she came to New York to support me when I was trying to get my career started. She applied for a job at American Express, and she was so cute and pretty they made up some receptionist position for her. She worked every day and brought home money so I could study and audition."

"In retrospect, I didn't like my job a whole lot," Midge admits. "But I wanted to go to New York and be with you in that wonderful little sublet in Greenwich Village."

"Where all we had to do was water the African violets for forty dollars a month."

"Then the sublet ended and we basically had nowhere to stay except that horrible hotel for a couple of nights."

"At Fifth Avenue and 5th Street," Dixie remembers.

"We put a chair under the doorknob."

"Do you remember that terrifying mouse in the closet?"

"Oh, Dixie," Midge sighs. "You always were a scaredy cat. When we were real little you'd ask me to go upstairs ahead of you because you were afraid. On the other hand, when I was in seventh grade and you were in ninth, I was deathly afraid of spiders, and you came along at a picnic and wildly chased some friends who were scaring me with a spider. We've always taken care of each other."

"You came to New York to save me when my first marriage was breaking up," Dixie reminds her. "I called and said, 'You must come.' You took your two little children, got on the plane, and when I came home from my soap opera, there you were."

"That was so different from the other time we lived in New York," Midge recalls. "This time you had a posh apartment, and we both had little children who were at a wonderful age to do things with. The circumstances were unfortunate, but we actually had a lot of fun, just the two of us together again."

"And you, looking after me in a big way." Dixie rubs her sister's arm. "I can barely talk about how much I love you without going into tears, into big middle-aged weepers."

"I feel like you are an extension of me, though we are quite different," Midge says. "You seem to think whatever I do is grand, and I get the vicarious excitement of being out in the world from your being there for me. Do you want to tell our dream?"

"You mean about our long-range ambition?" Dixie asks.

Midge nods.

"Well," Dixie pauses and takes her sister's hand. "When we get to the rocking chair stage, we plan on living in very close proximity, either side by side or in the same house."

Just like they were way back in McLemoresville, giving tea parties among the peach trees.

"Would I have a baby for a best friend? I'm not sure," Julie says, patting her belly. "But I had no reservations about doing it for my sister and her husband.

"Some people who have heard what I'm doing have said to me, 'There is no way I could do something like this for my sister.' I can't understand that. To me it seems, gosh, well why wouldn't you, if that's what your sister and her husband need? I knew how badly they wanted a child and they couldn't have one. If it took me to do it, that's fine. I don't know what kind of relationship other sisters have but this seems normal to us. It's just not a big deal."

These sisters tend not to be demonstrative about their affection for each other. When someone once suggested that Julie was presenting Janet with the ultimate gift, she replied, "It would embarrass me to think of it that way."

At the time this photo was taken, Julie, a lieutenant in the United States Navy who teaches in the ROTC program at North Carolina State, was one week away from delivering a baby she offered to make from her own egg and a sperm donated by her sister Janet's husband.

"We were in the kitchen of Julie's apartment just after swimming at her pool," Janet recollects. "The whole family knew we'd been trying to have a baby for several years, and Julie just asked, 'Would you want me to have a baby for you?'"

Two years would pass before Janet, who has a doctorate in math education, was ready to consider her sister's proposal. By then, she'd been through the fertility clinic routine and thousands of dollars worth of low- and high-tech procedures, including in-vitro fertilization.

"I'd reached the point of being pretty down," Janet says, "when I read an article in a science magazine about depression being a signal for humans to give up things that weren't working for them and try other options. After eight years of trying, I figured maybe it was time to accept Julie's offer."

They had every intention of using a doctor for the artificial insemination, but ran into difficulty finding a physician willing to assist them. That's when Janet remembered *the turkey baster*.

"I was watching one of those horrible Geraldo shows about an older husband and younger wife. They couldn't have children because his sperm count was low. So they used the sperm of his teenage son. It was casually reported they'd done the fertilization with a turkey baster. I was in my data-clipping mode and filed that as an option. Turkey baster? Mmmmmmmm."

It's okay to laugh. At the time they thought it was pretty hilarious, too. Nevertheless, Janet and her husband went baster shopping at a kitchen supply store. Mark preferred a metal model, thinking it would be more sterile; Janet, concerned about her sister's comfort, thought it would be too cold, so they settled for a plastic bulb baster which they sterilized in their dishwasher. With the help of an ovulation kit, they figured out the right time of the month, and on the appointed day Julie came to their house.

"Mark did his thing," Janet says with a big grin on her face, "and he handed me the baster. I'd never used one and we hadn't practiced how it worked, so when I took hold of the bulb I accidentally squeezed it and half the sperm came out. I thought, 'well, so much for this idea.' But I gave it to Julie anyway and told her to keep her finger over the tip. We were all laughing."

Julie went into the bedroom by herself. "I didn't need any help. It was easier than putting in a tampon. Then I stood on my head up against the wall, and I played little mind games with myself not to get bored. After twenty minutes Janet came in and then we ate dinner."

"We were all making jokes about what a fiasco it was, such a comedy of errors," Janet says. "We called it premature basting." But they repeated the whole thing the next day, just in case it might work after all.

One month later, Julie's period was late. Despite two positive results with home pregnancy test kits,

Janet couldn't believe they'd actually been successful.

"I was sure she'd read the instructions wrong. After eight years and a turkey baster, it couldn't be this easy." A visit to the doctor's office confirmed that yes, it could. Janet remembers, "When Julie called me, I kept saying, 'You'll never have to buy us another present as long as you live. Not a birthday. Not an anniversary. Never.' "

One thing these sisters are very clear about is who the baby belongs to. "I've always thought of the baby as Janet and Mark's," Julie says firmly. "It will be my little niece or nephew."

"I feel Julie isn't just giving us a baby, she's giving a person a life," Janet says. "We're all very lucky."

Which reminds them of the wishbone story. Once when Janet was trying to conceive, she and Mark followed a special diet that required them to eat lots of poultry. Every weekend when Julie came to visit, Janet would roast a turkey and save the wishbone.

Mark refused to wish with her because he wasn't superstitious. So week after week, she and Julie would hold the wishbone, close their eyes, and make a wish.

"This is so silly," Julie finally said one night. "It doesn't matter who wins because we're both wishing for the same thing."

"Really," said Janet. "What's your wish?"

"I'm wishing that you and Mark get pregnant."

"That's funny," Janet said, laughing. "I always wish for a million dollars.

"And that is why," she says, "Julie got pregnant instead of me."

John Franklin Wittley was born weighing in at seven pounds, twelve ounces. Both mothers and child are doing fine.

Linda and Susan:
The Karlin Sisters

"Do you like it?" Linda twirls in front of her sister, showing off her bridal gown.

"It's gorgeous," Susan gushes. "Wow, you even have cleavage."

"Were you excited when you first saw me? Was it scary?"

"Why? You're the one who's getting married. Actually, it is kind of overwhelming. My little sister a bride! My god, I guess this means that one of us is really a grown-up person now."

"You could borrow this, you know."

"We should all be alive that long."

"I want you to know that I don't believe you can replace a sister with

a husband. I'm not a person who takes away people in my life. I'm adding Peter on, and I expect you two will love each other because I love you both."

"I don't feel like Peter is invading my territory. It's more like I'm gaining a new friend. But I guess this means we won't sleep together anymore when we come home for Thanksgiving."

When, as youngsters, Susan and Linda were moved into their own perfectly-furnished bedrooms, they continued to sneak into each other's beds because being separated felt like punishment.

The only time they had a major competitive clash was in high school. Susan, a senior, and Linda, a sophomore, were up for the same role in the school play. "I wanted that part and tried like mad to undermine Linda's confidence because I saw her as serious competition," Susan remembers, still obviously feeling guilty. "One night at the dinner table she started to cry. 'Susan, we're sisters. What are you doing? We're not supposed to undercut each other. We're supposed to support each other.' I looked at her and it was devastating. She was right and I felt terrible. I apologized and said, 'Go knock 'em dead in your audition.' Linda got the part and I was disappointed, but I was also excited for her. She was my second choice."

Today it's often Linda who basks in Susan's achievements. "When Susan has an article published in *The New York Times*," she says, "I gain by that because she's a part of me. And it's exciting when she calls and tells me she's going off to the Cannes Film Festival or she was just at a party with some TV star and they hit it off because they both came from New Jersey. Other people don't get that from their sisters. All they do is call each other and swap recipes."

Their mother has a simple theory for why her daughters developed respect for each other instead of jealousy: "Unconsciously they staked out territories that each one could excel in. They sort of made their own spaces, their own places." Susan became a writer, an actress and a stand-up comic on the west coast; Linda, a marketing and meeting planner on the other side of the country. But emotionally, they will always be next-door neighbors.

"You bring a constant sense of fun and craziness into my life," Linda tells Susan. "A gym teacher in high school once asked me what it's like living with you. I said it was a continuous vaudeville show. If you weren't my sister, I'd have missed the show."

"And you give me a solid foundation and a sense of when I stray too far from the norm," Susan replies. "I know I have a best friend for my entire life who is never going to go away.

"Maybe we could still sleep together when we come home for holidays. We'll just ask Peter to come join us."

The Luong Sisters

Saan Luong had a dream. For thirteen difficult years, this dream was her only relief from the harsh reality of her life. Then one day, her dream came true—and she discovered that what she'd been nurturing was more of a nightmare.

In 1979, Saan was a skinny 10-year-old living in Vietnam, the youngest in a desperately poor family of five older sisters and one brother. At that time, the Communist rulers decreed that upon reaching 15, a child could be taken away to work for the country. Some children were never seen by their families again. Saan's brother had already been arrested by the Communists for carrying forged papers, and had escaped to China. Saan's parents decided to try to save their littlest girl by pirating her out of Vietnam before the government came to look for her.

"My mother told me we were going to visit my grandmother in the country," Saan begins. "But the way we went was different, and she said we were going to stop at a another place first.

"Just before we leave, everybody is unusually nice to me. My sisters buy me things, get me clothes, and I'm thinking, 'wow, this is a big change.' Usually they're too busy to pay any attention to me. They even take me out to a restaurant, and we were so poor we could never afford to go out to eat. They know I'm going away. I don't.

"We got to this place and my mother left me with her friend and said she'd be back soon. But the boat had to take off before she came, or else the Communists would catch us. My uncle was supposed to be with me, but he got arrested. He yelled at me to run to the boat. I didn't know what was happening or where I was going. I just did what he told me. There were a hundred and fifty of us on a seventeen-foot boat. All I can see are strange people and I don't understand anything."

Four other boats, fleeing at the same time, capsized. Their survivors were loaded onto Saan's boat and the food supply thrown overboard to accommodate the added weight. "I am terrified," Saan remembers. "You can't move. You sit with your knees up to your chin. You go to the bathroom right there in your clothes because if you get up you lose your seat. I'm the only one that doesn't have my family, and I am thinking, I'm the youngest one, why me? Why not my sisters? They must not like me."

The refugee camp on the Malaysian border where Saan was eventually interred housed seven thousand people. She was squeezed into a tiny hut with twenty-four others—including her mother's friend, whom she finally found.

"There was stink and worms. But we were lucky; it was far from the smelly bathrooms. I cried a lot."

After several months she managed to get a letter to her parents, who thought she had drowned. In their reply, she learned why they'd sent her away and how they hoped she'd have a better life. Frightened and isolated in a crowded, filthy camp filled with strangers, their way of "saving" her seemed like a cruel joke.

After a year and a half in the refugee center, Saan was relocated to Hawaii, where the daughter of her mother's friend lived. It was there she discovered that her brother had made his way to Philadelphia.

"It was, oh my god, so great! I will see my brother. He can take care of me. All that stuff. But when I move in with him, it's not like that. He's about twenty years older than me. He gambles a lot and he doesn't care about me at all."

When she reached 14 and could lie about her age, she got a job in a Chinese restaurant and moved in with a friend.

"Every day I go to school until two and I go to work until nine P.M. And I think how different my life would be if I had my sisters with me. I watch my friends with sisters close to them, and it breaks my heart. Always I think if my sisters were here it would change everything because sisters always know what we want.

"I pray for my sisters to come here so they could help me and do the things older sisters are supposed to do for younger ones. I write them how I wish they were here so we can do things together and talk like American sisters do. They write back and say the same. So all the years go by, and I have these hopes and dreams that one day they'll come and we'll be so happy."

It didn't seem like such an impossible dream. Her brother had applied for visas, but then had let the paperwork lapse.

"I found a teacher who would co-sign so we could get the family out fast, but my brother wouldn't give me the information I needed. 'What do you know? You're the youngest and I'm the oldest. I know everything.' One year passed. Another year. Another year. Finally I just start writing to everybody." Saan wrote to the embassy in Thailand, to her senator, to the U.S. State department, to one congressman after the other. Finally, in the fluorescent glare of an airport lounge, she was reunited with her parents and three of her five sisters—fourteen years after their separation. When she'd left them, she was a frail, sheltered Vietnamese child. Now she was a 24-year-old American woman with a son and a daughter of her own.

"I was so happy and excited. I had my children draw the welcome signs in Chinese and Vietnamese. But once I see them in the airport, it's like they just see me yesterday. I cry, but there are no hugs or kisses. Not like a normal family. I think deep down inside they must be happy, too. But they don't show it. My dad and mom look glad to see me, but not my sisters. They don't seem to want to know anything about my life without them all these years.

"Then the next day, they tell me they want to go home. Later I learn they had been writing to my brother that they don't want to come, but they write me different letters because they don't want to get me upset. It costs five thousand dollars to bring them here. I don't have money to send them back.

"They're always complaining. In Vietnam, they were spoiled. They never work a day. My mother took care of them. Here they have to work in a sewing factory. They say it's tough and boring and cold. Oh my god, this is not what I expected! I think my sisters will listen to what I have to say. They'll help me take care of my children so I can go back and get my high school degree. But nobody even wants to stay with me. I understand my parents are old, and old people always want to stay with a son. My brother doesn't treat them nice, though. But why don't my sisters stay with me? My husband and I have a basement in our house that we fixed up so nice as a bedroom for them, but they won't come.

"Every time we see each other, we can laugh and talk, but once we go down to something personal or deep, the party's over. It's doesn't matter how much older they are—one is 35, one is 34, and one is 38—or how young I am. We're supposed to talk to each other and take care of each other. But my connection with them has a line. We go so far and that's it.

"Part of me is in pain; they don't know anything I'm feeling. It hurts to see the three of them very close and good friends. They know everything about what the other wants and likes, but they say I can never be a part of them because I'm too American.

"Maybe it would be better if they hadn't come at all, and I just had my dream of what it would be like if we are all here, sisters together. Inside of me I love them. I try to think they love me too, even though they'd don't act like they do. I have to accept that I can't change them. I can't force them to be what I want. I can't make them love me. That was just a dream."

Alexandria, LA
September 11, 1942

Dearest Sisters,

So sorry I had to fib to you. I'll explain later. Harold and I were married this afternoon at 12:29 in the Jewish temple. The ceremony certainly was beautiful. I wore my blue pinafore dress, freshly laundered, of course. My bouquet—a beautiful white gardenia—was in my hair, and my ring is a gorgeous gold band from Kress: ten cents and a penny tax. You see, instead of getting any old thing, Harold and I decided to wait until we come home. Isn't Gerry Sills a darling name? Well, that's the last of the Adelmans. What a crew!

. . . Now for some important instructions. I have no clothes down here. Please send the following immediately (kinda ironic to be the owner of a lingerie shop and have no trousseau). I need: a. alligator bag. b. blouses—good condition ones only. c. grey flannel suit with bag to match. d. Chinese P.J.s and also my yellow midriff.

. . . Anne dear, you owe me three bucks. Well, kindly reimburse. . . .

Now Millie, dear, here's where you come in. I'm asking you to take over for me for about two weeks at the shop until Harold gets a furlough. Naturally the salary of twelve dollars per week is very little but perhaps I can arrange to send you about five more. . . .

So things are quite wonderful. . . .

Much love,
Sister

Millie, Gerry, and Anne: The Adelman Sisters

Fifty years after Gerry Adelman eloped with Harold Sills, she marked her golden anniversary by staging the wedding she'd never had. In an armory decorated with World War II memorabilia, she served an officer's mess that included mashed potatoes, succotash, and jello to two hundred guests instructed to come in clothes they would have worn circa 1942. As her own private joke, she dressed in a ruffly Southern confection that might have come straight from Scarlet O'Hara's closet—her teenage fantasy of how she had wanted to look as a bride.

Anne's reaction to Gerry's bash was, "That's my sister! She's nuts."

Millie, the emotional one of the trio, got weepy when she read the invitation. "I'm finally going to see her married. How lucky." So she packed her bags in California as Anne did in Florida, and they flew to Philadelphia for their sister's belated wedding. Before the ceremony, they sat down and reminisced. As often happens, their remembrances of things past didn't quite jibe.

Their mother died during kidney surgery when Millie was eight, Anne, six, and Gerry, just a year old. "We were staying with grandmother while mother was in the hospital," Millie recalls, "and we never left." Father was only an occasional presence. "When he was around," Millie says, "he was the best father he could be."

"That's interesting," says Anne. "He was the worst father I could imagine."

"He took us to dinner or the movies every Saturday night," Millie answers.

"That's not my recollection at all," Gerry says.

"You didn't go," Millie explains. "You were too young and Grandma wouldn't part with you. You were always greenish-looking and skinny, and she worried neighbors would think you weren't being taken care of."

"My memory," says Gerry, "is that Anne was the conservative of the family, Millie was the fast one, and I was just the baby."

"Millie wore too much lipstick and I didn't approve," Anne defends herself. "So I let her know."

"You still do," Millie says with a sly smile.

"I was more practical," Anne goes on, "and always the best-looking one."

"But I was the Miss America, the fancy one," Gerry interrupts. "Harold says they must have taken the wrong children from the hospital because we're all so different. Anne is into golf and bridge. I'm much more aggressive and worked in the fashion business all my life."

"We don't share common interests," Anne says. "Probably we wouldn't be friends if we weren't sisters. But I can't imagine going to anybody else when I'm in trouble."

"That's because it never mattered to us who had what," Millie says. "Whoever needed, got."

"It's still like that," Gerry says. "I remember when I was 15, Millie had an outfit she'd never worn. I can still picture it. And she let me wear it first. I never forgot that. Now we share problems. Though I've been married fifty years, I think my sisters know me as well as my husband, maybe even more, because they remember me as a child. It's a very close relationship."

"We're all totally devoted to each other," Millie chimes in.

So devoted that when their grandmother died, 17-year-old Millie, who was then making twenty dollars a week selling cosmetics, rented an apartment, moved her young sisters in with her, and assumed the role of caretaker. "Because I was the oldest, and my grandmother brought us up saying, 'One for all and all for one.' That's exactly it."

"I have no recollection of that," Gerry muses.

"You were seven years younger," Millie says. "I remember lots of things you don't. I bought a budget envelope, put five dollars away for rent every week. We got two cents spending money every night and a nickel for ice cream cones on weekends."

Gerry stops her. "That reminds me of a story that has always stayed with me because it foretold what we'd become. It was in the '30s. Times were very bad. I was 10 maybe?"

Millie cuts in. "You gonna tell about the green shoes?"

"No. No. What I recall is that Anne and I had a dime. I wanted to spend it and she wanted to save it. Doesn't that describe our personalities? But the dime rolled into a grate and that ended the discussion. I think about that incident a great deal."

"Oh," says Millie. "I thought you were going to tell how you bought those green high heels for school."

"Gerry didn't buy those shoes for school," Anne corrects her. "She had a date and bought them to match an outfit she borrowed from me."

"Well, at least we've never had a fight so serious we stopped speaking," Gerry says.

"Never. Never. Never," comes from Millie. "But we don't disagree as sweetly as you make it seem."

"And now Millie has this new line," Anne complains. "She says, 'I'm 80 years old and no one can tell me what to do.'"

"She's been saying that since she was 60," Gerry teases. "The truth is we've never had any sibling rivalry between us since we each have something: Anne has all the money, I have all the glamour, and Millie has all our love."

"That makes me the richest," crows Millie. "I love my sisters far before anybody or anything. Always did. And even more so now." Then, still the emotional one, she pulls a tissue out of her pocket to wipe her teary eyes.

"There was a polio epidemic—it was August, 1954, a year before the Salk vaccine came out—and the municipal hospital needed nurses," Rhea begins. "I'd just graduated from nursing school and agreed to work there for just six weeks until my position in a private hospital started. On September 21, six weeks to the day, I woke up feeling sick. The doctor said I had a deep-seated flu. My neck hurt. My thighs hurt. My back hurt. Everything hurt. I was quivering all over, but I had no fever, and I knew something wasn't right. You don't quiver with the flu. The following morning my fiancée came to see me, and I told him to let me brush my teeth and wash my face before he came up. I took about four steps and that was the end. I was totally, completely paralyzed. I couldn't close my eyes, couldn't breathe, couldn't unbend my arm."

By the time the polio ran its course, Rhea was left paralyzed from the waist down, unable to walk. The disease would reshape every aspect of her life. And in ways she could never have imagined, it would affect her relationship with her sister, Nancy.

Rhea's sister, younger by six years, remembers that initially, she felt inconvenienced by her sister's polio. "When you're 16," Nancy recalls, "you're so wrapped up in your own world. I knew Rhea was in a wheelchair and would never walk, but I had no idea what that implied for the rest of our lives." And because this wasn't a family that talked about feelings, neither of the sisters knew how to express their raging emotions. "There were so many undercurrents then," Nancy says, "and no way to vent them."

"I was bitter, miserable, frustrated, and angry," Rhea says. "I wanted to die, to kill, to maim."

"She'd never been easy," Nancy says. "Her place in the family had always been as the demanding one. Now she'd sit like a queen in this Barcalounger my parents bought her, expecting people to come to visit and choosing to see this one, but not that one. She wasn't the benevolent person she is today. Everybody kind of tiptoed around her because she was rotten. And understandably so. I remember in high school I'd be washing the dinner dishes and thinking, 'Goddammit, why can't *she* do

Nancy and Rhea:
The Lemmerman
Sisters

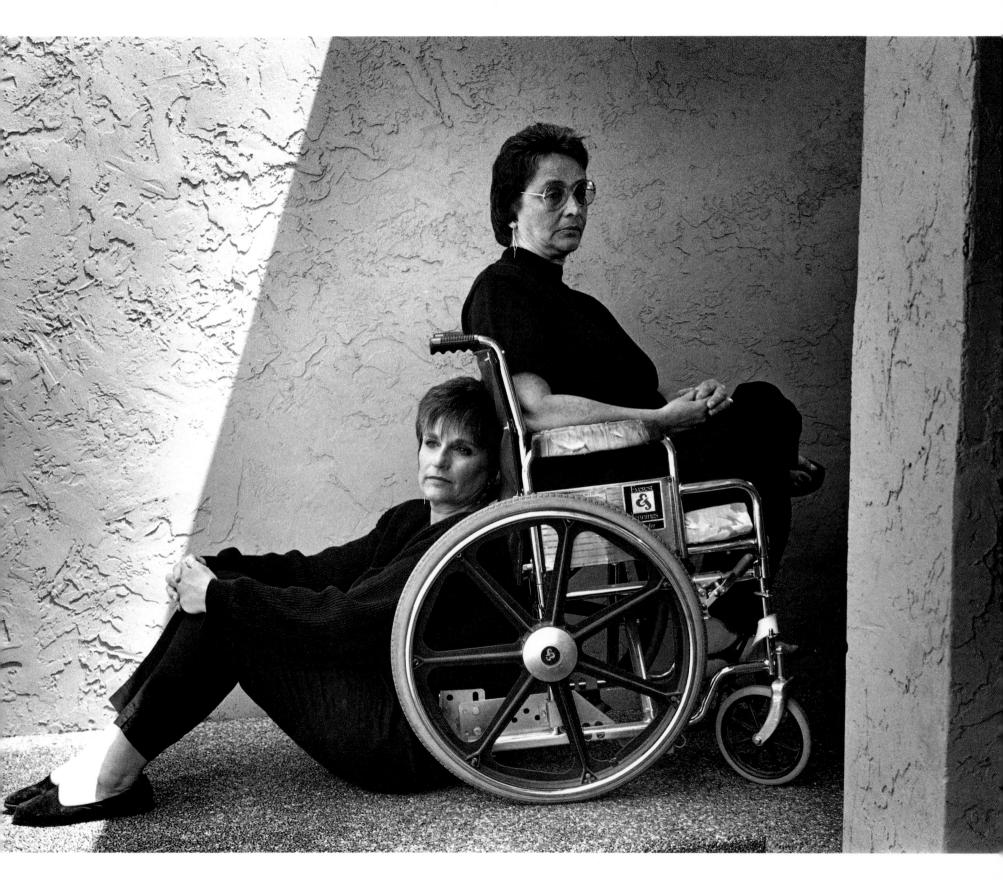

this, just because she's in a wheelchair?'"

"I took advantage of my condition," Rhea acknowledges.

"And I'm sure I resented you," Nancy admits. "Remember when I had to go to a fancy birthday party and I didn't have a formal dress? Mom was never terrific on getting us clothes, and she said I could borrow that strapless blue gown you'd worn someplace when you were engaged. You got so furious when I put it on. I can hear you screaming in your chair, 'I don't want to see you in that dress.' But I wore it anyway because I had to."

"I was so jealous of you. And so depressed. I wanted to be married and have an apartment and go shopping at the A&P and push a baby carriage like all the girls in my crowd were doing. But my engagement had been broken off and because everyone I knew was where I wanted to be, I couldn't tolerate seeing anyone."

By that time Nancy had gone away to college. "Mother would call and say, 'Nancy, Rhea won't see a soul. She won't go out. You're her only friend. You're the only one she wants to be with, so you have to spend time with her.'"

"That's when my sister became my lifesaver," Rhea says, squeezing Nancy's hand. "All during college, she gave me one weekend a month. I'd learned to drive a specially-equipped car and I'd go to Douglas [then the women's college of Rutgers University in North Jersey], pick her up, and we'd be off to New York for the weekend. We saw every show, went every place for dinner, rolled and strolled up and down Broadway and the Village. And once a year we'd take a major trip. We drove to Florida twice and one time flew to California."

"That last summer we went away I was starting to be serious with my boyfriend and was very reluctant to go," Nancy admits. "But Mom said I had to, so I did."

"That tells you about the character of my sister," Rhea points out. "I never knew that hesitation or felt it, and believe me, in my situation your antennae are out all the time. One of the reasons I love being with Nancy so much—and that goes for now as well as thirty years ago—is that she's totally non-judgmental. She just accepted me. Nothing was ever a big deal. Like a few years ago when I wanted to go to Europe. I knew it would be difficult, and someone in my physical situation can't put that on a friend. So I asked my sister."

"Of course I said yes. You paid for it!" Nancy quips.

"But that's not even the issue. I couldn't have gone if you didn't go. There were plenty of physical obstacles on that trip, but you made everything easy."

Rhea made it easier for Nancy, too, by evolving into a strong, financially independent woman. "It finally got to the point where I couldn't stand it at home anymore," she says. "I was dying. I had to get out. I took five hundred dollars, my car, and two pieces of clothing and moved to Florida to get my college degree. I even stole Nancy's bathing suit top because I didn't own a strapless bra. It didn't bother me, then, that I stole it. I just figured I needed it. But when I think about that now, I could vomit. To steal from her when I loved her so much. I've lived with that for years."

"The fact that it still bothers her tells you about the character of *my* sister," says Nancy.

Rhea remained in Florida and created a productive life for herself. Today she heads a prestigious program at a rehabilitation hospital. Nancy is married, has three children, and lives in New Jersey. Both sisters have master's degrees in educational counseling.

The key to their successful adult relationship is balance. Nancy has never felt she gives more to Rhea than she gets in return.

"Growing up, I was always treated very much like the baby in the family," she says. "On some level, I still am. And I kind of like that role. Rhea was and always will be my older sister. Despite what happened, our roles were never reversed. She takes complete responsibility for herself, and I feel like she also looks out for me. I'm very well taken care of."

Rhea begins to weep softly. "Nancy knows how much I adore and respect her. I worry about her. She had a mastectomy and, and. . . ." She is unable to complete her sentence.

Nancy picks up the thread of Rhea's thought. "Rhea knows I feel exactly the same way about her. It really alters the relationship when one of the siblings no longer mirrors your life. I doubt we'd have had this intensity if Rhea didn't have polio. It also helps that we have the same attitudes."

"After what we've lived through, her cancer, my polio, we just don't take everything so damn seriously," Rhea says. "I think we're able to cope with what's happened to both of us because we don't sit around and kvetch."

"Even though we find most things really funny, we're very realistic," Nancy says. "We just know what we have to do, and we do it."

"I was a few months from taking my vows when Mary knocked me off my feet and said she was joining the order, too. Of course I was so happy, but I can't say I thought much about what it would mean to our relationship as sisters." For Catherine and Mary, both Sister Servants of the Immaculate Heart of Mary, becoming Sisters did not create the sisterly love they have for each other. That existed long before they went into the convent.

"In certain ways, this has brought us closer together," Mary says. "We're both teachers, so we have that common interest, too. Because we live the same lifestyle, Catherine is more understanding of some conflicts I may have. And there are secrets, especially of the community, that you can tell your sister because she's a sister and she's *your* sister."

"Mary doesn't hesitate to do something I'd only think about," Catherine adds. "She acts on my thoughts. Like when Mom was so sick, I was thinking it would be nice to pray aloud with her—and Mary just started doing it. Prayer is a very spiritual thing and because we share a bond that might be a little deeper than you'd have with anyone else, our prayers can be deeper, too."

Their spiritual connection remains secondary to their family connection. While they have lived for more than twenty years in a community of devoted women, it's to each other they turn first when they need support.

"More important than anything is having your sister with you when there is family suffering," Catherine says. "It divides the pain and trouble in half when you carry the burden together. We don't live in the same convent and sometimes we wouldn't see each other, except when we were at home taking care of our parents. There was never any question but we'd both show up in a crisis and that made things much easier. That's where our closeness comes from."

Mary agrees. "You ask me if I feel lucky that my sister is also a nun? No, I feel lucky my sister is my sister. That is what matters to me. That we both are nuns is only an added blessing."

Sister
Catherine and
Sister Mary:
The Glackin
Sisters

Donna, Debbie,
and Shirley:
The Masiejczyk Sisters

When Shirley looks at her sisters, she sees reflections of herself. It's not just that they all have fair skin, blonde hair, and the same green eyes rimmed in blue. Or that they pierced each others' ears in elementary school. Or that when they shop separately for birthday cards, they often buy the same ones. And it's not even that the three of them wear the uniform of police officers. It's something much deeper.

"You know those television commercials where somebody stands in front of the mirror and the mirror talks back? That's what a sister is," Shirley says. "A part of yourself that responds to you. You can see it and feel it. This person you grew up with and shared everything with, who has your genes and your blood and is so much like you, yet also different. I draw great strength from that. You can't get the same thing from friends."

"Friends are friends, but there's always a line you don't cross," Donna explains. "With us there's never any line. We did plenty of fighting growing up, and we probably tell each other off every day. We're very critical, but it doesn't mean anything. Being sisters gives us lots of freedom to air our opinions, but there's an understood obligation to be careful not to hurt."

Debbie adds, "Friends support you in a different way. When I was going through my divorce, my friends felt sorry for me and wanted to take me out drinking and stuff, but my sisters were there for me night and day. Whatever happened to my marriage, I knew my sisters would always be my sisters. They weren't going anywhere."

"I tried to get my husband to understand that when we were picking godparents for our daughter," Shirley says. "I wanted to choose Donna, who was single at the time. My husband got this idea that godparents should be married. We went back and forth and finally he picked his sister and her husband. A few years later they were divorced. I never let him live that down. He should have let me pick Debbie because she'll be around forever. You can depend on that."

Joining the police force was Shirley's idea, which isn't all that surprising considering she's the eldest and the one who's always told the younger

sisters what to do and how best to do it. "You know how it is with the big sister," she says. "You're like the mother and you can't help doing a lot of what they'd call meddling."

Debbie was still a senior in high school when Shirley, who'd already been out in the work world for six years, dragged her along to take the entrance exam for the police academy.

"I didn't want my sister to make the same mistakes I did, like not going to college or getting stuck is some dull, dead-end secretarial position," Shirley remembers. Debbie agreed to go along, "just to keep Shirley quiet." Four years later, Donna left her clerical job and joined them. "I didn't like feeling left out."

Sharing the same career gives these sisters more to talk about—"We always seems to end up discussing work," Shirley says—and more to fight about. Shirley is a supervisor, which tends to slant her perspective. "Our differences on the job can cause friction away from work," Debbie says. "We're always telling Shirley at home, 'Remember, you don't have your lieutenant bars on here.'"

Being policewomen definitely gives them more to worry about. "I remember, I'd been on the force about four years when Donna came into the department,"

says Debbie. "I knew there was danger out there, and she could get hurt. I'd had my face slashed by a hostile mental patient, and I'd had to shoot an angry husband who attacked me on a domestic violence call. When Debbie got assigned to a busy district without many officers, I found myself monitoring her all the time on the police radio. Once, she called for help, and my partner and I raced there from our district. A cop who arrived right after us said he had never seen anybody take six or seven stairs at a time like me— that's how fast I went up the steps. When it's your sister at risk, you worry. You really worry." Since then, they've made it a point to specialize in different areas.

If, on the one hand, these sisters are a source of concern to each other, they also provide a unique emotional safety net.

"I can't imagine what it would be like not to have a sister to support me, to tell me the truth, to be there for me whatever it was I needed," Donna says. "When we were kids, we took it for granted that there was always a sister on the other end of the teeter-totter. Now I realize what that really means. How do people get through life if they have to go to a playground by themselves?"

Sheryl and Nancy:
The Glass Sisters

So tell us true, Sheryl. Aren't you just a teensy, weensy bit jealous that your sister Nancy Glass hosts a nationally syndicated television show and gets all the attention?

"Absolutely not," Sheryl insists. "Being on the stage and doing plays was always what Nancy liked. I never had that desire. She's happy doing her thing, but I have *my* thing and where I live in Boston, I'm known for being me. I remember when Nancy started in television, I was working in the management program at Ann Taylor. This woman walked into the store and insisted she'd seen me on TV, on *Evening Magazine*. 'Listen,' I kept telling her, 'if I were on *Evening Magazine*, would I be here waiting on you?'"

"My parents never made a big deal out of what I do for a living," Nancy dives in. "They care more about what kind of wife and mother I am—and if I keep a nice house. They're very hard to impress. A few years ago I hosted a show that aired in some markets at midnight. My father asked me, 'Why are you on at midnight?' I told him, 'Dad, we're number one in the market.' He gives me this deadpan look. 'Honey, they're using you for a night light.'"

Nancy and Sheryl may live very different lives, but they look alike, sound alike, and even dress alike without planning. "Our tastes are so similar," says Nancy, "that if I like a movie or book and she doesn't, I think, 'Now wait a minute. Did I *really* like this?' I'm a very strong person and make important decisions every day, but if my older sister doubts a decision of mine, then I tend to doubt it, too. She's my barometer."

Sheryl screws up her face in one of those you've-got-to-be-kidding looks. "Puh*leeze.*"

"Well, it's true. You were the star in the family, Sheryl. There are hundreds of pictures of you in the family album and only *one* of me."

"Right, Nancy, and you've been making up for it ever since."

They play off one another like a comedy team, giggling at inside material. There is no space in this relationship for anything as petty as envy.

"You have to understand that Sheryl's the big sister and I always looked up to her," says Nancy. "As kids we did everything together—only she did it better. I always thought she was prettier. More stylish. More graceful. She was this petite and perfect person when I was a 12-year-old with size nine shoes. So she got to wear Weejuns and my mother made me wear white bucks."

"That's why I didn't want to share your clothes."

"You didn't like to share anything. Remember when we had those dogs and Mom said, 'Sheryl, you must *share* the dogs with Nancy.' So you said, 'All right. She can have the back halves.'" They fall apart laughing.

"Nancy was such a tomboy, a real magnet for trouble. Always getting hurt. When she was four she already knew the way to the doctor's office. Our father used to call her Captain Klutz."

"Because I could fall off a carpet."

One memory triggers another and suddenly Nancy

says, "This is exactly what sisters are about. We've shared our lives for over thirty years. That is *something*. You can tell your sister things you can't say to anybody else. I can say the dumbest thing to Sheryl or ask her which fork to use without embarrassing myself. When my husband, whom I adore, has been with me as long as my sister, maybe then I'll tell him some of the things I tell her."

"With a sister you never have to censor your words," Sheryl says. "We talk about everything and nothing, from lipstick colors to serious things like politics and war."

"We're on the same wavelength," Nancy says. "I could shop for her, and she buys me the best presents. We even have this nutty thing about food. In our family we always eat before we go to a party or restaurant, just in case we don't like the food when we get there. I mean, who wants to end up eating the bread? My husband cannot understand why I do this, but Sheryl thinks it's perfectly natural because she does the same thing."

"If I stop to wonder why we're so close," Sheryl says, "I think it's because of our parents' expectations."

"My mother was an only child," Nancy continues, "and she'd go on and on, all the time, about how 'Someday I won't be here; you'll only have your sister. So you have to be friends and love each other.'"

"Yeah," Sheryl says, "and remember how we'd roll our eyes and scream, 'Get her away from me!'"

But if you hear the same message long enough, eventually it sticks. "By college we started to understand," Nancy continues.

"Once we were no longer living on top of each other and had established our own identities, Mom's words took on another meaning, and we realized exactly what she meant. So I figure we'll end up in the nursing home together. Sheryl will still be telling the story of when I was 13, and the counselors at summer camp thought I was smoking cigarettes, which was forbidden, and they sent me home. After that, wherever we went, Sheryl would say, 'This is my sister, Nancy; she got kicked out of camp,' and I'd burst into tears. I was so humiliated."

"Oh Nancy, I can't believe that still bothers you."

And they dissolve into a fit of laughter at another family memory that only the two of them understand.

Janice and Elizabeth:
The Coffey Sisters

For the first eleven years of her life, Janice Coffey's sole siblings were all brothers—a fraternal twin and three older boys. She was especially close to the brother who was fifteen years her senior—the one who bought her the most wonderful little outfits, read her stories, and played dolls with her. Then, when she was four years old, he suddenly vanished, like a drawing on her Magic Slate. For the next seven years, their only contact was a monthly telephone call.

"My mother used to make me go through this ritual," Janice remembers. "She'd say, 'Your brother's on the phone and you can speak to him if you promise not to cry.' I cried a lot because I missed him. Nobody would say where he'd gone. There was this cloud of shame, like he had cancer or a terminal disease that nobody dared talk about."

One day, without warning, her mother revealed the family secret. "We were in the kitchen," Janice recalls. "My father left the room, and, as tactfully as she could, Mother told us that our brother was no longer our brother; he was now our sister, Elizabeth. Mom tried to explain the sex-change process and how she'd supported Elizabeth through it. Dad hadn't wanted us to be with her—maybe he was afraid it would rub off or something.

"My immediate reaction was a little resentful—*that's* the dumb reason you've been keeping us apart all these years! All of us kids pressed for getting together right away. I was especially excited, because I'd never had a sister."

The reunion was scheduled for a big party that Elizabeth was giving to celebrate her 26th birthday. Except for the new bumps on her chest, Janice didn't think that Elizabeth looked all that different.

"We rebonded instantly," Janice says. "To me the whole thing, honestly, was no more than a name change. I was so happy to have this person back in my life, it never really fazed me. Gender wasn't the issue; the person was the issue."

"Who I was—and my relationship with Janice—held far more importance than what I was called," Elizabeth says. "Though I was born genetically male, I've always been who I am now, which is female. When little boys reach their teen years they're supposed to go through some sort of physical metamorphosis that turns them into little men. Well, it didn't work out that way for me. By the time I was 19, the only way I could relate to myself in a sensible manner was to have all the pieces fit. So I became, for lack of a better term, one of the original Johns Hopkins kids."

Twentysome years later, whatever angst Elizabeth suffered at the time of her sex-change surgery has faded. She married, and even her father has come to accept her as fully as her siblings have. But clearly, the easiest part involved changing from Janice's brother to Janice's sister.

"Quite frankly," Elizabeth says, "I think we always related as sisters. I came back into Janice's life at a time when I was able to enrich her and myself through our relationship. If Janice were not my sister, she'd be my friend. We have so much in common. Both of us care about music, painting, reading. And then there were all the sister things we shared."

"You bought me my first junior prom dress," Janice reminds her, "and taught me how to wear make-up. We did all those arts and crafts things—ceramics, jewelry-making, needlepoint. Everything you were interested in, I had to know about. I don't think I'd be as politically or socially astute if it wasn't for your liberal, feminist views. It helped immensely to make me a more well-rounded person."

Couldn't Elizabeth have brought most of those qualities to Janice if she'd remained her brother?

"I don't think so," Janice says. "I have a wonderful friendship with my brothers, especially my twin, but it's not the closeness that sisters share. No one knows me like Elizabeth does. You can just totally open up to a sister. When I was little, I had great fun playing football and stuff with my brothers. I even joined the Boy Scouts. But when my big sister came back in my life, I finally had someone to talk to about girl things. I couldn't tell my brothers, 'I think this guy is cute' or ask, 'Does this dress look okay?' or, 'What color stockings should I wear with this outfit?' Elizabeth was what I needed."

Elizabeth also feels "enormously close" to her brothers.

"Quantitatively, we probably share as much with the boys as we do with each other," she says, "but what we share is different. I feel safe with Janice. When she says, 'How are you?' I know that I don't have to say, 'I'm fine.' Our conversations are emotionally-based rather than fact-based. We can be more intimate."

"She's constantly in the back of my mind," Janice says. "I'll see something, and if it's got Elizabeth written all over it, I have to get it for her."

"That reminds me of the bracelet story," Elizabeth says. "You must have been 12 when I came home one weekend from New York and pulled out of my suitcase a diamond and jade Victorian bracelet that had been given to me by a guy I was dating. 'Oooh, are they diamonds?' you gasped. I put the bracelet on you and it hung way down on your little wrist. You were fascinated by it, and, without hesitating, I gave it to you and told you to put it away because someday you'd grow into it.

"It's so obvious to me that when your sister loves something, you give it to her because she's your sister. I know that explanation sounds trite and sappy. But for me, that's just the only reason I ever need."

"The greatest tribute I can pay my mother and her two sisters is that from witnessing what they have, I feel a keen sense of loss that I never had a sister of my own. If I'd been that lucky, I'd have known exactly how to do it, because Minnie, Dotty, and my mother, Bloomie, were the best pattern-makers in the world. Too bad I never got to make the dress!"

Those eloquent words from Bloomie's daughter, Linda, describe three women who formed an exclusive mini-unit within a family of seven sisters. They've never dwelled more than ten minutes apart, and in 1970, when Dotty's husband wanted to retire to Florida, she refused to move until her sisters promised to follow her. Ironically, these three intensely devoted sisters had only one child each, but that meant, according to Linda, "That we all had three mothers." That vantage point gave Linda a unique opportunity to observe this remarkable four-score-and-still-flourishing relationship.

"Not until I became a young mother and a lonely adult living in a city away from home," Linda begins, "could I understand this wonderful connective tissue among them. How totally they share their lives. They told all, heard all. Enjoyed each other immensely. Had an incredible amount of companionability and a no-holds-barred commitment to intimacy. Never go to bed angry. Never bear a grudge. God forbid an unspoken anger or an unexpressed resentment should grow like a fungi into some poisonous plant. When they did argue they were outspoken about their disagreement, but it was carefully controlled. Nobody ever hung up a telephone. The most threatening thing in the world to them would be the loss of each other.

"What probably served as an escape valve was gossip. If one of them had a tremendous problem with the other, the way to deal with it and get rid of the pressure was to tell the third who went back and told the first. By the time the whole process went around, the tension was defused. The message got through and any ugliness was blurred.

"They came from a rollicking, bursting-at-the seams household full of women. There were two pianos, laundresses, boiling pots of starch, ruffles, curling irons, you name it. Apparently my grandmother managed to make each one of these kids feel like an individual. They never fell into a collective soup. They all felt special. Each has whispered to me at different times, 'I was grandpa's favorite,' or 'I was grandma's favorite.' That, I think, is what has enabled them to remain so totally accessible to each other. These sisters are like an immutable law of the universe that nothing could destroy. Nothing. Frankly, I think their marriages helped too. If they had married men who were emotionally demanding, I don't know if they'd have had as much energy left for each other. Sisterhood was much more rewarding, intimate, and sensual than marriage.

"Behaviorally they were quite different. My mother, Bloomie, was always like Rosalind Russell in *The Front Page:* Snappy patter, fast-moving, fast-thinking, enormously productive. A hard-boiled, hard-bitten dame. A terrific broad.

"Dotty, the clubwoman, had some kind of mythic vision of herself as a Southern belle.

"Minnie was a live wire, very bright, very compassionate. Soft where my mother was hard. Creative where my mother was linear.

"Certainly there have always been things about one another that have driven them crazy. To this day Minnie and my mother still complain about how long Dotty takes to make a decision, how unbearable it is to shop with her, because she's so fussy. Then my mother and Dotty complain how Minnie can be so obstreperous. And Minnie and Dotty complain about

my mother's tongue when what they want to say is that she is a mean S.O.B. Then they feel guilty, so they'll say she has a heart of gold—it's not *what* she says but how she says it. You see, loyalty is the leitmotif of their lives.

"And gratitude. They are enormously grateful for what they have. They know it and say it. And they are incredibly courteous to each other. Growing up in our houses it was classic to check in every day. I can still see my mother, home from work, making dinner. Phone starts to ring. Dotty checking in. Minnie checking in. Even today, my mother and Minnie live in the same apartment complex in Miami, see each other every day, and still they kiss walking in and out of a room. For a number of years, we lived next door to Minnie. She'd call my mother from her office to say, 'I'm going to stop at the bakery before I come home. Do you need anything?' My mother would say—I can hear her now—'Pick me up a rye bread. Sliced, without seeds.' Okay. Minnie arrives with the rye bread and my mother is instantly in her purse. 'Fifty-nine cents. Here it is.' That's just one example of how they were very careful with one another. Meticulous. Debts were recorded and paid but never thrown in anybody's face. Never. Never. Never.

"They need each other like light and air, but at the same time they're very independent, very proud, very cognizant of boundaries. When one of the children suggests that it might make sense if they got together and shared an apartment, they throw up their hands

in horror—nothing mock about it—and all say, 'God forbid. Can't think of anything worse.' Yet they're also interdependent. My mother is the last driver and primarily the doer. She complains, feels anxious about her capacity to keep doing, feels exploited. But I tell you she'd shrivel up without being needed by her sisters.

"My god, what an incalculable relief it is for the children that they are there to take care of each other. Dotty was mugged a few years ago and as a result of injuries she sustained had to move to a retirement community nearby. My mother put in untold hours of paperwork dealing with her insurance, paying her bills, et cetera. Do you think her son—who is chairman of the psychiatry department of UCLA—would have gone to Florida for eight weeks to do her checkbook?

"I carry two pictures of them in my mind. One is at my cousin's bar mitzvah. My mother is at the piano. My Aunt Minnie's got the maracas and my Aunt Dotty has a drum or something. They've got wastebaskets on their heads. Their stockings are rolled down, skirts pulled up, and they are having one helluva time. Then, sometimes, I picture them lined up and they're all old. All gray. All weathered and wrinkled, but above all, together. Together. That's the word. The only word. Together in body and soul.

"Just look at them. The panorama of what they've shared. They've had an ally, a best friend, a gal pal, a cheerleader in their corner, a helpmate, a caretaker throughout the entire course of their lives. Who am I going to have when I'm 82? My then 60ish daughter will be busy with her own life issues. Without a sister, who will I have to check in with? The desk in the lobby?"

Tangra, Karen, Claudia, Linda, and Aulana: The Pharis Sisters

P ut the five Pharis sisters alone in a room and you've partially solved the energy crisis. The electricity they generate when they get together could easily satisfy the power needs of a small planet. Aulana Peters was the first black lawyer appointed to the Securities and Exchange Commission, Linda Munich is public affairs director for WPVI-TV in Philadelphia, Claudia Pharis is a policy analyst with a Harvard MBA, Tangra Allen is a community activist and grant writer, and Karen Owens works as a direct mail account executive.

These sisters live in different parts of the country and don't see each other as often as they'd like. But there's constant phone contact and conference calls whenever one of them has great news to tell. When they do get together, they invariably recall the family stories that form the tight warp of their lives: The time Aulana whipped Tangra for playing with matches, but protected her by not squealing to Daddy. When Claudia got mad at Linda and destroyed her very best favorite most wonderful peasant blouse. How Aulana refused to apologize for kicking apart a jigsaw puzzle Karen had just about finished. The time Linda applied for a camp job and was told there were no other black counselors: "That's okay," she said, "I'm not prejudiced." That particular story still breaks them up.

These sisters lend resonance to the phrase *separate but equal.* "I am from a family of five sisters," says Aulana, "and we all act like we're only children, which says worlds about how our parents nurtured us to be sole and unique."

"That's for sure," says Claudia. "I got a beating every day and Aulana never did."

"Because she didn't deserve it." Linda pipes up, and they burst out laughing again. "We are a tremendously competitive family but I can't say we were ever jealous. At least not in the traditional sense."

"Well, of course, growing up, my sisters each had something I wanted for myself," Aulana admits. "When I was a gawky, gangly teenager I would look at Linda and envy her beauty. When I struggled to get a B+ and wanted an A in calculus, I wished I had Claudia's enormous brain power. Karen has this amazing capacity for love and patience. And Tangra is the most artistic. We all dabbled in dance, music, and painting, but I coveted Tangra's talent."

Somehow, what could easily have been petty jealousy emerges as tremendous admiration. Claudia appreciates Aulana's graciousness. "She was mommy number two to all of us and handled that role with such ambassadorial aplomb."

Aulana nods. "I never resented taking care of my sisters while my mother was working, but I think they're the reason I have no children. When the time came to have babies, I'd already raised my sisters, so I simply had no curiosity what it was all about."

"I think we all see each other pretty much the same," Tangra says. "Karen has this personal sense of order—I swear she was born with clean, straightened drawers—and, as an administrator, I could use some

of that. Frankly I was so different, such a nonconformist, I sometimes thought I was adopted. Finally my mother sat me down one day and said, 'Why in the world would I adopt another daughter when I already had three girls?'"

When asked to describe their roles in the family, they all have the same answers. It's agreed that, in birth order, Aulana is the group adviser; Linda, the nurturer; Claudia, the energy force, the most playful, and the favorite of the nieces and nephews. Tangra, the one who marched in Selma, is their conscience. And Karen is the glue, the one who calls everybody and remembers the birthdays.

Rather than feeling stifled by sibling rivalry, these sisters revel in it. Karen says, "Except for being the baby and having to wear hand-me-downs—remember those blue coats with the lace collars that wouldn't wear out?—this all-female group has always been tremendously reinforcing. You know how there are times in life when you need someone in your corner. Well, with five sisters you get to pick and choose because some are better in a particular corner than others."

Beyond that, these sisters hold up mirrors to each other for what it means to be female, and the reflections aren't clouded by the tensions of a mother-daughter relationship. "No matter how disparate we are," says Karen, "having four sisters gives you role models to learn how to become a woman."

Their one complaint about growing up in a houseful of women? "We had only one bathroom and Daddy always got first dibs." Their parents ran an orderly, traditional home where dissent was permitted only within a framework of understood obligations: Always show up for dinner, exhibit proper table manners, and talk during the meal. They were required to say "Good morning" every morning, "Good night" every evening, and to greet people when they walked into a room. But above everything loomed the unspoken rule, "Thou shalt love thy sister as thyself."

"We always thought," says Claudia, "that being the Pharis girls was the greatest blessing on this earth. There is nothing I could do, no disagreement I could have that would make my sisters not love me. We belong to each other and that is inviolate. We each contribute to the solidity of our bond by being there when we're needed. By carrying our own weight. You don't mess with that kind of stuff. You invest in it."

Sandra, Georgette, and Wendy: The Wasserstein Sisters

"How are we alike? Hmmm, let's see," muses Wendy, the playwright, on the subject of the sisters Wasserstein. "How about we have beautiful rosy skin, thick blonde hair, and no hips?"

"We have narrow cheekbones?" Georgette, an innkeeper, suggests.

"And thin arms," says Sandra, a high-powered banker and business consultant. "You and I are very proud of our thin arms."

"And we don't like scary things," Georgette continues. "When the music gets scary on a TV show we all leave the room."

"Do you like amusement parks?" Wendy asks.

"No, I hate them," her sister replies.

"And I think we all hate beets," Georgette says.

"I certainly don't like beets," Sandra agrees. "Do you like beets, Wendy?"

"I'm so amenable that I would eat them if I were forced to. But they're not as bad as those drinking eggs Mother gave us for breakfast." She turns to Sandy. "Speaking of food, remember when you came back from living in England? I was at the June Taylor School of Dance and also studying at The Yeshiva. I was pretty much a believer then. Anyway, mother gave you money to take me to Howard Johnson's and Radio City."

"Wait a minute," Sandra interrupts. "It was *my* idea to take you out. Mother may have given me money afterwards."

"But you were supposed to take me to Howard Johnson's."

"No, I just said I was taking you to dinner and a movie."

"Well, you took me to The House of Chan and we saw this movie called *Expresso Bongo* with a dancing scene where the girls were wearing little plaid kilts and had no tops on. Then we had coffee in the movie lobby. I found this totally startling."

"Probably because at dinner I ordered shrimp in lobster sauce and spareribs, which certainly weren't Kosher."

Retelling tales from their book of memories is something all sisters love—and the Wassersteins are no exception. Theirs was a rollicking, boisterous household (three daughters and one son), governed by the dictum that success comes from high achievement. When the kids weren't excelling in school, they were performing original shows in the living room.

"When we took car trips," Sandy remembers, "instead of listening to the radio, we sang camp songs and show tunes." And, as if on cue, they launch into a lusty rendition of "A Cannibal King with a Big Nose Ring," complete with hand motions.

"There were such large personalities in our family," Wendy says, "that I think I got along by being funny and sweet enough so that everybody would leave me alone. You had to stake out your own territory. My feeling has always been, 'If everybody's in Louisiana, then get yourself on a horse and go west. Why would you even bother with Louisiana at all?'" Her role was beloved baby of the family.

"Wendy and I shared a room, and she would jump into my arms every day when I came home from school," recalls Georgette, who is six years older.

"You didn't think I was so cute when I spilled ink on your college application," Wendy reminds her.

"And to punish me you locked me outside to get bitten by the squirrels and die from rabies."

Georgette, given the nickname "Gorgeous" by their father, embodied for her sisters what it meant to be feminine. "At eight, she was already elegant. *And* she had a clean neck," Sandra says with mock exasperation. "Mother always threw that up to me."

"And mother would say to me," adds Wendy with a giggle, "Look at Audrey Hepburn. Doesn't she look like Georgette?' I'd say, 'Yes.' In my mind, Georgette was very glamorous. And Sandy was the sophisticated big sister."

"I'm very conscious of being the big sister," says Sandra, thirteen years Wendy's senior. "In fact, my managerial style is modeled on having been the big sister. It's made me a very good coach, a mentor to younger people coming up."

Wendy credits her sisters with being her models for the myriad possibilities open to women. "They've shown me that women can have their dignity and do so many different things. They can own inns, or be executives. I always loved going to Sandy's office because in television or movies you never saw women in big offices like hers. And when I was in college at Mt. Holyoke, I would visit Georgette, and there'd be all this warmth with her home and kids. So I instinctively knew that women were valuable in all kinds of ways, because I grew up with it."

"I think my sisters have shown me how to live," Georgette says.

"Yes, of course," Wendy nods. "It has to do with that awful word, *values*. I think about sitting in your room when I was young, asking you if so-and-so was a nice person and sharing thoughts about what it meant to be a nice person, a good friend. That is something very basic I got from my sisters. And what I'd like to have from you now, Georgette, is that outfit you're wearing."

"Oh you can't," Georgette exclaims. "It's my gorgeous outfit."

"Well," says Sandy, "I might like to have Wendy's talent."

"Not me," Georgette answers. "I'm happy for Wendy to have the talent and to be related to it. I'm sincerely proud of both of my sisters."

"I feel blessed," Sandy says, "to have two people in my life who have to take me as I am, whereas the world doesn't. Back in the touchy-feelie era of the '60s, I was pressed by my company into attending a week-long, mostly male, executive self-awareness seminar. It was all about bonding and being supported by your T-group. By the end of the week, these men were talking about this having been the major experience of their lives. I mean *major*! I couldn't understand how could this be so profound for them. They were rich, successful, famous, married. Then I realized why it hadn't been so powerful for me. I'd been walking around with my own permanent T-group for years. Me and my sisters. With the exception of my children, I prefer their company to anybody else's. I feel very attached to them. Very big sisterly. Very. . . ." and she is too choked up to finish.

Wendy, in a soft voice, fills the silence. "I am very grateful to my sisters for teaching me what I know about people. For showing me different ways to grow. For never having to worry whether they'll show up for me. I'll never forget the opening night of *The Sisters Rosensweig*. This was a play I'd written about sisters, and here were *my* sisters with me. Sandy was sort of organizing people, saying 'Mother will sit here, and so-and-so will sit there.' Georgette was being charming and lively. And I was hiding. I thought, well, there you go. That's us. We're being just who we are. It was wonderful."

The three of them sit quietly for about thirty seconds. Then they break into smiles and begin to sing, "A Cannibal King with a Big. . . ."

Katie, Charlene,
and Julie:
The Cunningham
Sisters

The moment frozen in this photograph will always evoke a treasured memory for Charlene, Julie, and Katie. They've just returned from a perfect vacation, one they could not afford financially, but could not afford to pass up emotionally. They'd recently heard the news they'd most feared: Charlene's breast cancer had begun to spread, and the prognosis was not good. Without hesitation, they borrowed the limit on their credit cards and fled for a week to a rented villa in the Caribbean to be alone together, as sisters, one more time before Charlene's health started to decline.

Unexpectedly, the trip helped Charlene plan her funeral. "The idea came to me after we went snorkeling one afternoon," she said. "I was floating and looking at the spectacular sea life around me and I just wanted the current to take me away. I felt I was home. That's when I decided I wanted to be cremated and have my ashes spread out in the ocean. I don't want to be buried in a casket, because I don't want a place for my family to come and cry."

As children only fourteen months apart, Katie, Julie, and Charlene had been raised like triplets. (There is another sister, ten years older, but they've never been close.) "Three peas in a pod," their mother called them. They were given their first bikes on the same day, and, together, were allowed to stay up past nine o'clock for the first time.

"We lived in the country," Charlene explains. "If we wanted to go out and play, we didn't have anybody else, so we relied on each other for entertainment. We had to get along. We biked and hiked and rode horses. Even though we fought, we knew we'd always be there for each other."

As is the case with many sisters, the ride got bumpy in their teen years. There were fierce fights, especially over clothes—shared by the sisters, who were all the same size. Often Charlene and Julie would gang up on Katie, provoking new arguments. By their college years, feeling suffocated by their intense closeness, they drifted apart, but kept up with each others' lives through reports from their mother.

"I can't quite say how we came back together," Katie muses. "All of a sudden I identified that something was missing in my life: my sisters. I guess we just needed a little space to get rid of those adolescent resentments. When I look at other sisters who have terrible relationships, I think it's because they couldn't get past those petty little things that happen growing up. Now at least ten times a day something reminds me of my sisters and reminds them of me."

"We also learned what was out of bounds," Charlene says, "and how to make up afterwards. Just blow off the fight and never hold a grudge."

When they finally held a post-college reunion at the Jersey shore, they fell right back in love. Katie remembers, "I looked around and thought, 'My god, we're all adults now. This is our first adult woman vacation.' It was very significant. We had our own money and our own jobs and were really close again. I thought it was so great to be together. I imagined that we'd be doing things like this the rest of our lives. Then, six months later, Charlene got diagnosed."

Breast cancer often runs in families, but it doesn't usually show up first in a youngest daughter. Charlene was 25 when she first felt the lump. She went to the hospital right away. A needle aspiration and an ultrasound yielded little information, so a biopsy was scheduled. Julie, who works as a radiation technologist in the hospital, got the report first. "It's about Charlene," the doctors said when they called her in, and she thought, "Oh shit. It's bad. Real bad." It fell to her to tell her sister that she needed a mastectomy.

Julie knew Charlene was scheduled for a perm and she intercepted her at the beauty shop. "On my way over I thought about using a gentle approach, but then I thought, 'This is going to be an ordeal. Hard. There's no way I can lie to her, so from here on in I'm going to tell her absolutely everything. I have to be tough.' But when I saw her coming down the street, I went numb and I wasn't sure I'd be able to get the words out."

They walked to a park nearby. "You're not sick. You are fine," Julie told Charlene. "There's nothing wrong except this lump and they have to take it out."

Charlene heard the words like a death sentence. They both started to cry.

The next victim was their mother. Her tumor was not as large nor as aggressive as Charlene's, and required only a lumpectomy. But that was when Julie and Katie, a registered nurse, began to panic, and on the advice of physicians decided to have their breasts removed as a preventive measure. The sisters, with their marvelous sense of humor, kept each other smiling with boob jokes.

"We talked about getting our boobs knocked off," Charlene recalls. "It's good to be able to take things lightly because they are just boobs, you know, and there's more to life than body and boobs."

For several months they focused on their mutual surgeries to divert attention from Charlene's condition. "I was reassured by seeing Julie's," Katie says. "We communicated every step of the way. What do they look like? How do they feel? We'd always talked about everything. Sex. Our husbands. We had no secrets." In the meantime, Charlene moved in with Julie (who was coordinating her treatment) and her husband and started chemotherapy. Everybody feigned optimism until the cancer recurred and there was little left to hope for.

Julie began to feel overburdened. "Help me, Katie," she wept. "I can't be as strong as I have to be." Katie got on a plane from California and came to Philadelphia to stay with her.

These sisters, who have always talked about everything, are now talking openly about death. Charlene tells her sisters how grateful she is to them for giving her an outlet to share her pain and fear. "There's nobody I can be more comfortable with, just be myself."

Katie asks Julie, "What the hell are we going to do without her? It'll be so boring. We'll be incomplete. We balance each other so well."

Julie fights despair. "She's our adventurous spirit. Who's gonna get us to try new things, loosen us up?"

Recently, Charlene told Katie she's going to leave her an expensive diamond ring from her canceled engagement. "I want you to have it," she said. "Will you wear it for me?" Katie could barely answer. "I just don't know. I don't know if I can."

Charlene believes she has lived before and will live again. "I'm most sad about leaving the ones I love because I know how much they'll miss me." When Katie heard about a medium who channels spirits of the dead, they chose a special word for Charlene to use from the beyond to establish contact. And, true to form, it was something raunchy.

Should Charlene manage to get a message through, her sisters already know what they want to hear. "That she's happy. That she knows we love her. That there is still a connection between us."

Kim, Sandra, and Sheryl: The Blackie Sisters

Dozens of impediments could have prevented the Blackies from being friends—different interests, personalities, lifestyles, and even different countries. Two live in Canada, one in California, but they rarely write or talk on the phone. Family news tends to get circulated indirectly through calls to their mother. But the shared history of their youth is enough to make all their differences unimportant.

"We're sisters," Sheryl states quietly, knowing that those words obviate the need for further explanation.

Still, Sandra, who lives three thousand miles away, embellishes her sister's thought. "No matter how old, how young, how good, how bad—no matter what—your sisters are there," she says. "We have no choice, because we will always be related."

Kim, the youngest of the three, concurs. "Well, anybody can see that: we all have fat ankles."

These sisters have plenty of good memories—camping, fishing, riding, sharing clothes, sneaking beers and cigarettes—and plenty of bad ones, too. "Our stuff is there all right," Kim acknowledges, "but we act like it's way in the past. Water under the bridge. We talk about what's current and focus on the present. Even if we fight, the next time we see each other, we act like it never happened."

Even the old resentments, especially between Sandra and Sheryl, burn less intensely now that the sisters have reached their thirties. "We were only two years apart," Sandra says, "and my parents dressed us the same way. People thought we were twins, and it was awful. I wanted to be me. I wanted people to like me alone, and I hated that my mother was always pushing us together, making me take Sheryl everywhere."

"We always ended up fighting," Sheryl says, "because I could talk to Mom—I was her favorite—and the minute Sandra tried to talk to her, they'd be yelling and screaming. That caused lots of friction between us. And Sandra was a terror. She caused a lot of trouble."

Sandra was wild: drinking and drugs, running with a fast crowd, minor clashes with the law. "I was always a rebel. For a lot of my life—but no more—I've been involved in pretty hard-core addictions."

Sheryl hated Sandra for tearing the family apart. "She was older; I couldn't tell her anything. It was so difficult to sit there and watch what was happening. If I did say something, she basically told me to go to hell. Teenagers are like that. But now," she says strongly, "I'm very proud of her."

"You are?" Sandra asks with surprise.

"Yes. I've seen you hit bottom and get back to where you are today. Totally clean. A champion body builder. Healthy. You've got direction in your life. That's quite a change."

Sandra sighs and shakes her head in wonder. "Out of everybody in the family, I'm always most nervous about seeing you, Sheryl. Kim and I have always had our athletic interests in common, but I thought you didn't care about my lifestyle, which is the thing that's most important to me. You didn't seem to have any interest in my bodybuilding. It never dawned on me that maybe the distance between us came from my old addictive behavior."

As the sisters talk about the past and present, it becomes evident that they still crave each other's approval. Kim admits that before seeing Sandra, she was worried about getting into shape. "Yeah," Sheryl says, "when we get around each other I start thinking Kim's thinner and Sandra's this health nut. Me, I just come home from work, sit on my butt, have coffee, smoke cigarettes, and try to relax my brain."

"I don't think we want to be *like* each other," Sandra suggests. "It's more the feeling that if your sisters don't accept you as you are, who will? I'm sorry sometimes that we don't go out of our way to be in contact more. Funny, isn't it, that it doesn't really make much difference where we are or what we do. We're still bound together. Still connected.

"If one of you committed murder or won a million dollars or landed on skid row, it wouldn't change one thing."

Clare, Chris,
and Jeanne:
The Evert Sisters

Chris Evert—the number-one world-ranked tennis player for seven years—has beaten just about everybody she's ever played. But her roughest matches may have been against her younger sister, Jeanne.

"There was a time when I was 17 and she was almost 15—we're two years and nine months apart—that we were pretty close in ability. We'd both been tops in our age groups. We spent every day on the tennis courts and traveled the junior circuit together. The tough moments came when we started on the pro tour. It got pretty strained. Tennis was my security, the one area I wanted to be superior in, not only with her but with everybody. We played against each other three times in tournaments, and that was the sickest I ever felt in my life. On the one hand, she was my sister, and if I was beating her badly I felt sorry for her. On the other hand, if, all of a sudden, she started winning a few games from me, I felt threatened. It was the worst feeling ever."

Fortunately, their competition ended before the attachment between them frayed. "It's easier to have one big win than it is to stay winning," Jeanne explains. "There are a lot of elements that go into making a champion, and I might have had one, but I didn't have all of them like Chrissy. She's just a lot more competitive, and I came to accept that. My dad used to ask me, 'What are your goals?' and I would answer, 'To be happy, to get married, and to have a family.' I reached a point where tennis wasn't giving me that happiness."

By then, a third sister had joined them. Clare was born when Chris was 13 and Jeanne, 10. "She was not so much our sister as she was like a daughter," says Chris. Despite the differences in their ages, the girls grew up to become best friends.

Clare and Jeanne developed a close rapport when Clare reached high school and Jeanne, newly married, returned to Fort Lauderdale from Canada. Jeanne took a position coaching Clare's high-school tennis team and drove her baby sister to tournaments while their parents were away watching Chris play in matches such as Wimbledon. Clare and Chris bridged their thirteen-year age gap after Clare graduated from

college and began working as a tennis pro at a club in Aspen, where Chris owns a home and spends much of her time. (Her other house is in Boca Raton, not far from Jeanne.)

Today the sisters' relationships form an equilateral triangle where the connection between any two points is as important as the connection among the three. The lessons they teach each other as adult sisters are far different from their old court secrets.

"Maybe growing up, I was the leader," Chris says. "But now I think the roles are reversed. I look up to Jeanne because she's always been the perfectionist in the family. Whatever she did, she did really well. Whatever I did, I did okay but never as well as she did. Except for tennis. Because I travel so much, I haven't been much of an expert on domestic issues. I see the way she is with her kids, her patience, and how she spends time with them. She is Miss Chef—makes these beautiful dinners—and always has her house immaculately cleaned."

"This year I just couldn't do Christmas dinner like I always do," Jeanne interjects. "The family got so big, up to thirty people, and my house is one-third the size of Chris's so I asked if she'd mind having it. She said, 'Okay, I'll just call the caterer.'"

They all laugh, and Chris continues, "Both of my sisters are doing things I never did. Clare graduated from college, has a place of her own at 25. I lived with my parents until I was married; one regret I have is that I never lived alone. She deals with her bills which I had an accountant do. So it's like I'm the young one. Clare is really a people-person, which I'm not naturally, so she's taught me to relax, enjoy life, and not get so intense about everything."

"We've all learned from each other," Clare says. "Being a people-person isn't the greatest thing in the world unless you've also got some of what Chrissy has. When I go out to play a match I can do it physically, but I can't focus or concentrate like she can. Nobody can think like Chrissy. One in a million has that talent she has. So you come to respect your sister for her strengths. And one of the things that's great about growing up with somebody so famous is that you get to see people for who they really are."

Chris nods her head and smiles. "So Mel Gibson walks into the tennis club and Clare is like, 'Yeah, Mel Gibson is playing here. No big deal.' Nothing fazes her."

"Right," Jeanne adds. "Clare is our free spirit. Chris and I are more traditional and conservative."

But there was nothing conservative about the way Chris chose to have her son, Alex. In 1988, she married sports commentator Andy Mill. When she became pregnant two and half years later, she decided she wanted her sisters right there with her in the delivery room.

"She told us in no uncertain terms, 'You're going to be there,' " Jeanne says.

"I flew down from Aspen and waited about ten days for her to deliver. Almost got fired."

"Jeanne's kids were adopted, and I thought she would like to see a baby being born, have that experience with me," Chris says. "Since I was also the first girl in the family to give birth, I thought my sisters should be there to support me. I wanted them with me—and my mom, too. I had a twenty-four-hour labor so it was pretty awful. They were all there with blankets trying to get some sleep. That experience brought us closer."

Almost as difficult as Alex's birth was choosing which of her sisters would be her son's godmother. "I tossed and turned for three months," Chris remembers, "worrying over whose feelings I was going to hurt. Maybe I wouldn't have another child. I didn't want to choose Jeanne just because she's the eldest. That would be unfair to Clare. She's an adult now, and I love them both the same. I wanted them both involved." Her solution perfectly reflected their relationship: she asked them to share the role and be co-godmothers.

As these sisters have matured from girls to women, the sport that was so central to their interaction has moved to the periphery. "Early on, tennis was our common bond," Jeanne says. "But it doesn't even enter into it anymore. Now it's marriage, children, home, religion, spirituality, so many things."

Kay, Loretta, and Loudilla: The Johnson Sisters

*N*ow y'all listen to this here story 'bout the Johnson girls and how they came from a farm in a windy corner of Colorado and done got themselves famous enough to be photographed by Avedon, written about in Time Magazine and booked for a guest appearance on "Hee-Haw." They can't sing a lick nor play no music neither, but they're best pals with Loretta Lynn and they chum around with all them Country Western stars. Even look like stars themselves with their big hair and cowboy boots.

What they do is run fan clubs. That's big stuff in these parts. They kinda stumbled onto it back in 1960. Loretta Johnson—she's the zaniest of the three, writes novels and says jest what she thinks—anyway, she up and wrote a fan letter to Loretta Lynn back when she was just an unknown playing clubs for fifteen bucks a night. Well, this was the very first fan letter she ever got and the gals started hanging out and helping out. One thing led to another and they hitched their wagons together.

As Loretta Lynn climbed the charts and became a major star, her fan club increased to more than five thousand members. Other fan clubs, noting the great job the Johnsons did for Loretta, sought out their advice. No sense giving it away, they thought. So they became consultants to the industry and founded the International Fan Club Organization, which has grown into a booming business with 320 members and a wildly popular annual dinner show just for Country Western fans. Along the way, the Johnson sisters have become something of a legend themselves, and today these queens of fan clubdom have darn near as many fans as the singers they promote.

Their business partnership is just a small part of why the Johnson sisters are as tight as three hens sitting on a single nest. In the fifty-odd years they've lived together, they've never been apart longer than thirty days, and that was when Loretta went to visit her Momma and lost weight pining for her sisters.

The girls were largely raised by their daddy, a powerful, beloved figure who passed on in 1987 as a result of injuries sustained in a head-on auto collision. The sisters mention him at least once every five minutes. "When we lost our Dad, a lot of people thought, 'Well, those girls are going to fold up,'" Loudilla says. "They misinter-preted what we were about. We were Daddy's pride and joy, but he made us stand on our own two feet. In our family we all take care of each other."

Daddy Mack Johnson farmed wheat on a seven-thousand-acre spread. Picking up the mail was a fifteen-mile ride; a quart of milk, a forty-two-mile round trip. By necessity the three sisters and their three brothers formed their own little community. By the time Loudilla was eight years old, Momma was gone, leaving her in charge. She cooked; the others split the chores of laundry and cleaning. They had a perfectly wonderful, though isolated, childhood and never felt they'd been cheated of anything. When Loudilla, the sharpest of the lot, graduated high school, she won two scholarships but used neither.

"It was like this," Loudilla says. "Loretta hated

school. I knew she'd quit if I left home. So I stayed, and she finished. That's how the fan club got started. We'd met Loretta Lynn, and I wanted a hobby, something to occupy my time."

After Daddy died, the farm became too much for the girls to handle, so they moved themselves and their business to a four-thousand-square-foot, decorated-to-the-rafters home in a suburb of Nashville. Barring marriage, which seems unlikely to them, they expect to live together happily ever after.

"I don't think any of us ever made a conscious decision that 'My sisters are more important than any man, so I'm not going to marry,'" Loudilla explains. "But men do seem intimidated by our closeness."

Could they imagine being separated? Just barely! Except for the fact that the younger sisters "lean on Lou more than we should," they go together like chicken and biscuits. Kay, the quiet one with a whispery voice as gentle as her personality, says, "It's so convenient and logical to live together. We enjoy it. It's other people that find us strange. Okay, strange in their world, but not in mine."

"To me," Loudilla says, "weird is sisters who haven't spoken in fifteen years. Or sisters who were good friends until their mother died and have fought ever since because one got the china and the other took the silver. Oh, lots of times I can hear those two saying, 'Keep away from Lou today cause she's bitchy and got her tail over her back.' But when we're mad, we talk about it."

"Daddy taught us," Loretta says, "if you've got something to say to somebody, you need to say it. If you don't, the problem festers inside and becomes bigger than it deserves to be."

"He was smart man, our Daddy," is Kay's contribution.

One time Daddy woke up 'round about midnight hearing all kinds of laughin' and chatterin' downstairs. He put on his clothes and tiptoed into the living room, carryin' his shoes in his hands. There, settin' on the sofa, were the three girls gigglin' and carryin' on fit to beat the band.

"Why, Daddy, what are you doing awake?" one of them asked, surprised to see him.

"I heard all this partyin' and I jest assumed we wuz havin' company," he said.

"Nope, Daddy. It's jest the three of us having fun all by ourselves."

In all these years, nothin's changed.

Kristin and Laura:
The Beck Sisters

"Is there anything I like about my sister? I don't think so," says 16-year-old Laura Beck.

"We're just not connected. Our personalities don't click. She's not the type of person I would hang out with. It's better if I stay away from her and don't get involved because I know we're going to have a fistfight or an argument that will lead nowhere. It would take a lot of work to build this relationship, and right now it's just not worth it to me."

The Becks are typical of many sisters who battle their way through their teens and can't imagine that they might ever become friends.

"I'm kinda jealous when I see other families where sisters sit and talk and the little sister looks up to the big sister as an example," Kristin, 14, says wistfully. "It hurts when your older sister doesn't like you and beats you up. You feel like you have no friends."

"It's not that I'm being a bitch," Laura defends herself. "But everything she does annoys me. She does stuff because she knows it will drive me nuts. She enjoys aggravating me."

"When you go and tell Mom I'm annoying you, I do it again on purpose," Kristin admits.

"Like the time you were sick and you kept asking Mom, 'When do I take my medicine?' I told you, 'You take it three times a day. It says it right here on the bottle: Once in the morning, once in the afternoon, and once at night. It's not that difficult.' But every ten minutes, it was, 'Mom, do I have to take my medicine yet?' Over and over. And you kept it up because you knew it pissed me off, didn't you?"

"Yeah," Kristin says. "Because you call me hunkachunk and tell me I'm fat. I know I'm fat, I don't need to hear it from you because you're skinny."

"I only do it for your own benefit," Laura retorts. "You eat constantly, every bit of junk we have in the house. And I wish you'd grow up and learn some manners. She's so gross."

"You can yell at me; I don't care. I can always get even by going to Mom and tattling on you and then you get yelled at by Dad."

Bicker. Bicker. Bicker. It never stops.

When the girls were younger they shared a room, and their mother had to separate them for fear they'd injure each other.

"It wasn't little fights," Laura says. "Every night we really beat each other up. We fought over any little thing. Basically, I'm fanatic about neatness and she's messy. Her stuff could pile up for years and she wouldn't care. Finally, I drew a line down the middle of the room and told her, here's your side. I'm not vacuuming it anymore."

Forget anything as sisterly as shopping together. "I couldn't shop with her," Kristin says. "She usually gets Mom to buy her the thing I would want, and if I pick something out for myself, she just goes, 'Yuch.'"

Laura rolls her eyes in exasperation. "We have totally different tastes."

Laura and Kristin have developed warmer relationships with other siblings, but those don't substitute for their failure to get along with each other. They're painfully aware of how sisters are "supposed" to behave and will admit a deep sadness over not matching the ideal.

"I feel bad that I'm not the big sister Kristin wants," Laura says quietly. "I don't give her much credit for things, like working hard when she does well in sports. I should be more protective. A big sister should show her younger sister how to act, what not to do, who not to hang out with. But I can't pretend to be that kind of sister for her, because I'm not a fake. And I know it hurts my parents. It would mean so much to them to see us get along. They feel they did something wrong bringing us up, but it's not their fault. I know everybody tells us, 'Someday you guys will be best friends.' It's awfully hard to believe."

In her own way, Laura misses having a sister she can depend upon as much as Kristin does. "Out of all the people in the world, sisters are the ones you are supposed to be able to totally trust and confide everything," she says. "But Kristin is such a different person from me, she wouldn't understand where I'm coming from. She's such a goody-two-shoes."

"How come you can tell your friends things you can't tell me?" Kristin asks plaintively.

"Because I don't care how other people look at me. But I do care how my own sister judges me. I don't want you to know my inner secrets, because I don't want you to see me as I really am. I just want to graduate high school, go away to college, and get on with my life."

"I'll be happy then," Kristin says. "Once you're gone, it will be my turn to be the oldest sister in the house. I hope that if we stay far apart for awhile, maybe there is a slight chance someday we could get close."

Bernetta and Margaret:
The Crommarty Sisters

"We never separated too much," Margaret reckons. "We's always been side by side. You know how it is when you got a younger sister and your father tells you to be together and love one another. In them days you did what you was told, so we never got too far apart. Never fought much either. What we gonna fight for? We was raised not to fight. Came up in the church and never knew much else."

Once upon a time, these eighty-something sisters did everything and went everywhere together. Now they go nowhere and feel blessed simply to still be together. Their parents are long gone; of the eleven children in the family—Margaret was the eighth and Bernetta the youngest— their only remaining sibling is a 95-year-old brother in a nursing home. Their husbands, divorced, are forgotten. "If they weren't right, I didn't stay with them," Bernetta declares. Neither has children. What they do have is a deep faith and an unconditional commitment to one other that makes it pointless to paraphrase the biblical question and ask, *Am I my sister's keeper?*

Margaret and Bernetta own one of four dilapidated houses that remain on what was once a stately block in a neighborhood of Philadelphia that has decayed beyond hope. The sisters' entire existence has been confined to the 10-by-30-foot front parlor since 1984, when Bernetta lost two toes to diabetes and with them, the ability to walk. "We eat here. We sleeps here and we doo-doo here." There is a commode behind a screen and a television set in the corner. A few pieces of faded furniture are draped with brightly-colored coverlets that Margaret crocheted in the days before her arthritis, when her fingers could still work the hook.

At 86, Margaret is five years older than Bernetta and, by comparison, relatively healthy. "I got bronchial asthma and lately my blood pressure's been jumping up on me, but I don't worry. The good Lord takes care of me, so I can take care of Bernetta."

"I'm gonna tell you, Margaret does *everything* for me." Bernetta says with a tired wave of her hand. "I sit in this chair. I can't go get nothing. She gives me something to eat. Helps me wash myself. I don't know what to do but love her."

Their daily routine rarely varies. Margaret rises each day around seven A.M., folds up the roll-away bed she sleeps on and wheels it into the front hall, where it remains until she pushes it back into the living room every night so her sister won't be alone. Then she prepares their breakfast from food a nephew brings once or twice a week.

"Bernetta don't like cereal, so I make potatoes and eggs, or hash and eggs. Maybe toast. Before we eat, I bring her teeth and some water to wash her mouth. I has to give her all her medications—three pills before she eats, for her sugar and something else, and four more after she eats. I clean up from breakfast, dusts a little, makes her bed. Then Bernetta needs to be washed. I can't get her to the bathroom. I bring in a pan of water, wash her down, and put on a clean nightgown and robe. I wash up the same way. Can't get in the tub myself 'cause I can't get out. Besides, if I went upstairs to shower and fell, who would hear me? I is supposed to soak her foot every morning in warm water and she should be greased all over 'cause she's so dry but I can't do more than her foot. Comes the evening, I read my Bible and pray."

"I'm always telling her sit down and rest. Seems there's nothing Margaret hates doing for me."

"Sometimes I say I ain't gonna do so and so, but I get right up and does it anyway. If I weren't here, I don't know where she'd be or who'd look after her."

Lately Bernetta's mind has begun to wander, making her dependent on Margaret not just for her medications but also for her memories.

"Did I used to sing in the choir, Margaret?"

"Yes, you surely did, honey."

"What did we sing?"

"We sang 'Jesus loves me.' "

And in reedy, off-key voices, they hold hands and sing, "Jesus loves me. Yes, Jesus loves me, for the Bible tells me so. Oh yes, God is real. He's real in my so . . . oo . . . ul."

Though the memories are foggy, Margaret and Bernetta love to talk about the past and sometimes even about the present. But they rarely talk about the future.

"Lots of sisters don't look after each other like we do, Bernetta."

"I didn't know that. Why not?"

"Because they wasn't raised like we was to stick together. We're blood."

"Yes, that's true. But we is *old* blood. And you wouldn't leave me nohow 'cause we always been close. Very close." Bernetta raises her index and middle fingers and squeezes them together. "This close," she says. And they both grin.

Irlene, Louise,
and Barbara:
The Mandrell Sisters

Barbara Mandrell was a five-year-old "only child" when her sister Louise was born, and she made it clear to her parents that she had no interest in sharing the spotlight. Her father, Irby, decided to try a little of homespun psychology.

"Louise had dark hair when she was born," Irby says, "and Barbara was blonde. When we brought Louise home I told Barbara, 'They must have given us the wrong kid. We don't have any black-haired children. This can't be your sister. I'll just flush her down the toilet.' I walked into the bathroom, closed the door, laid Louise in the bathtub and pulled the shower curtain.

"Barbara was screaming and crying outside, and as soon as I walked out, she found Louise, picked her up from the tub, and announced, 'It's okay. I want to keep her. I'll take care of her myself.' By the time Irlene came along eighteen months later, Barbara was so used to having a sister, she just took her in, too."

The Mandrell sisters have been lovingly caring for each other ever since. "We all feel special," says Louise. "I believe with all my heart that I'm the favorite in the family. I know Irlene feels the same way, and so does Barbara.

"We're all very comfortable with our roles. Irlene loves being the baby. She's really the family comedian and the best entertainer, on and off stage. I've always been Aunty Louise, the one the kids love and who takes them everywhere—the Girl Scout leader.

"Barbara was always the bossy big sister. 'Stand here, smile, do this.' She's in the center of things, very much in charge. At family events she drives us crazy with her camera. She takes all the pictures and we can relax, because we know the prints will come in the mail. She also happens to be very knowledgeable, and we listen to her because she knows what she's talking about."

During her long recovery from a nearly fatal car accident in 1984, however, Barabara assumed a different role in the family. In unexpected ways, that experience brought the Mandrell sisters to a new level of appreciation. "I was in Barbara's hospital room," Louise recalls. "She didn't know who I was and it was obvious already that she had a bad head injury. I held her down while the doctor set her leg, and that day changed our relationship.

"All of a sudden there was no one telling us what to do. I became the big sister for a long time. I was the one who organized the family. That was so hard for me because I never knew how important those things were or how well Barbara did them.

"For a long time I lost the sister I knew. She stayed in her house with the curtains drawn and wouldn't go out. Her personality changed. Then when she came back to herself and took over again, we went through another transition. I had to make room for her to be herself and she had to allow space for me. Strangely enough, through all of this, we became closer."

Without the active encouragement of her sisters, Barbara might not have returned to the stage. "After the accident, I thought I would never perform again," she says. "But my sisters were right there, urging me to listen to my father's advice. He said, 'Just get up there one more time and then decide.' They all supported me not to let the accident dictate my life."

Barbara says her sisters are unfailingly sensitive to her needs in all kinds of ways. "Louise and Irlene always say or do just the right things to make me feel better," she says. "When we were doing our TV show together, it was a very building time in our relationship. They were always worrying about my health, seeing that I ate enough. I'll never forget when a reporter came to interview us and asked about how we handled sibling rivalry. Well, we'd heard of it, but had no idea what it was."

"And you were afraid," Louise reminds her, "that people would think something was wrong with us because we don't argue. So you told that reporter we fight over normal sister things. And me, Ms. blunt Louise, said, 'No, we don't,' and right there we had our first argument—over whether or not we argue."

"Well," Barbara says, "I was thinking about arguments like 'Oh no, I shouldn't have this, you take it. It looks better on you.'"

"Like the mink coat?" Irlene asks. "This nice Italian man wanted to make Barbara a mink coat but she already had one. So she gave him my measurements instead of hers, and when the coat was ready, she gave it to me. Later when the man found out, he thought that was so nice he made another one for her."

As tight as the sisters are as a threesome—"When we're together as two, we're always worrying about the third," Louise says—they also make a point of carving out time for one-on-ones. Every January, Louise takes Irlene on a trip for her birthday. And sometimes, when Irlene is too busy for an outing, Barbara (her neighbor) will drop in, grab a dust rag and help her clean house.

"Once, I was living in California, studying acting," Irlene says. "My birthday came and I was feeling really lonesome for my family. My husband told me he was taking me to a restaurant that had a special room just for us. When we got there, two people were sitting at a table with menus in front of their faces, and I was annoyed because I thought we were supposed to be alone. Then they lowered the menus and it was Barbara and her husband, Ken. They'd come to surprise me. I started to cry. Both my sisters are big-hearted and generous in a million ways. They are truly my best friends."

While the Mandrells admit to being strongly competitive with each other in games and sports such as softball, golf, and target shooting, there is no competition in their careers. "It's not because we're so nice," Louise says. "It's because we had smart parents. When Barbara started out in show business she could not afford a band, and would not have had one, had it not been for Irlene and me."

"Barbara had married Ken," Irlene explains, "and decided to retire from show business and be a Navy wife. Louise said to me, 'Watch. She won't retire forever. We have to keep practicing our instruments so when she goes back, we don't get left out again.'

"One night we all went to the Opry and Barbara couldn't stand sitting in the audience. Pretty soon she was back on the stage. When she put together her band, Louise and I were as good as anybody—all that practicing paid off—so she made us her original *Do-Rites*. We toured all over with her."

Louise completes the story. "Later on, Irlene and I became successful because of the Barbara Mandrell TV show. We got her started, and she got us started. When someone is successful and you help them get there, you can't but celebrate your part in it. Our work gives us something extra to share.

"I've always been a little bit leery about explaining my love for my sisters in public because I don't want us to sound crazy, but there is a bond between us that goes beyond normal sisters. I think it comes from our love of God, from our parents teaching us to love each other unconditionally, and from sharing a business where we've helped each other and been there for each other."

If there is one complaint these sisters have, it's that their busy careers don't leave them enough time together.

"We decided to set aside once a year where we would go away, just the three girls," Barbara says. "No children. No husbands. We planned to go to Atlanta and thought it would be grand. Room service. Just us talking. Well, the three of us were asked to co-host an award show and the script needed our attention, so we used the time we'd set aside for each other to rewrite it.

"We're still trying find our three days together."

Nine-year-old Melba Smith and ten-year-old Clementine Moorman became sisters in this house when Melba's mother, a nightclub singer, married her accompanist, Clem's widowed father. The concept of "stepsisters" never even entered their family. "It would never occur to me to tell people we were stepsisters," Clem says today, and Melba agrees. "We just don't relate that way."

Clem remembers being thrilled with the news that she was gaining a sister. "I had just lost my mother and was looking for something to fill up that nice feeling again. The fact that Melba was almost the same age was nice, too. But when she arrived, well, we had to go through an adjustment. I was looking for somebody who wanted to go shopping and play dolls with me. Melba was a tomboy. Much rougher."

Melba nods, remembering the unhappy spirit she brought to their home in Newark, New Jersey, pictured here. "I'd been slapped around and beaten up a lot. I was bright but I'd been brought up to think I was stupid. I couldn't express myself. I'd never been allowed to. It was, 'Sit down and shut up, girl.' So I was very quiet and sullen. And here was Clemmie with this gift for speaking. She was so articulate, always reading books. Didn't like to be dirty and she couldn't fight for nothin'. But she could tear you to shreds with her ladylike attitude."

Clem's gentleness was exactly what Melba needed. "I would probably have been dead by now if this new family hadn't come along. I was already so convoluted, so bitter that I couldn't talk. A lot of my learning how to live came from watching and observing Clemmie. Her sweetness eventually healed me. She gave me the gift of her loving heart. To me, it was the difference between life and death."

"You couldn't dislike her," Clem says, smiling at the memory. "She was so bewildered, such a little prankster. There was nothing else to do but make her my little sister and love her."

"I think we really came together when we started being conspirators, the kids-against-the-adults thing," says Melba. "Because our parents were entertainers, they were away and left us alone a lot. When they did come home, it got to be a confrontation. Here we'd been taking care of ourselves just fine, and it was like, now you can't come back and tell us what to do. That really bonded us."

And bond they did. They went to their proms together. Sang spirituals around the piano. Fought over boyfriends. They made 1-2-3 cakes of flour, sugar, and water. "There was so much of each ingredient you died from cholesterol. Remember, Clemmie? And how we used to dress up alike and go to supermarkets and guess how many people would ask us if we were twins."

They were absolutely, positively, best friends, which may be why Clem took such pride in Melba's emerging talent: "She is not just an actress and a singer. Melba is a gifted, extraordinary musician. As a teenager she was totally absorbed in music. Practiced for hours and hours. She would willingly give up her social life to learn something on the piano. You could tell early on she wasn't going to lead a nine-to-five life."

So it was no real surprise to the family that though both girls became teachers, only Clem remained in the education field. Melba Moore moved up to Broadway, jumping from the chorus of *Hair* to the lead role. Then it was on to a Tony for her performance in *Purlie*—and a career as a recording artist and television star.

As the sisters' worlds diverged, their relationship suffered. Melba's dedication to her craft and her determination to succeed built a barrier between them. "Looking back," Clem says, "Melba's early days on Broadway were the best time of our lives. She was where I could lay my hands on her. I'd drive from Philadelphia to New York to be at all her openings. She wanted to share her good times and her good fortune. Seems like I saw her more then. But lately we just haven't been as close."

"My lifestyle has been so different from Clem's," says Melba. "Besides that, our living in different towns has made it difficult to be together."

"I don't think it's just about Melba being famous," Clem says sadly. "It just seems she doesn't need me anymore. Doesn't want to be with me, and that hurts. But that doesn't dispel the fact that Melba is my sister, and if she ever calls and says she wants me or needs me, I'm gonna be there."

"Would you only be there if I needed you? Is that the only way you'd be comfortable?"

"No," Clem answers. "What I'd really like is for you to think of me as someone who you just wanna be with when you have free moments."

"I hear you," Melba says. "I understand. If we're going to be tight like we used to be, I have to make more of a special effort. Call you. Have lunch with you. Make you a part of my routine and my life. I forget to do that."

"I'm making an effort, too," Clem tells her. "I'm planning to move back to New York so these things can happen. I can't think of anything that's more important to me. You know what I'm going through, my depression and all that, and I know what you're going through with your separation. That understanding is very deeply rooted between us."

"In the old days, Clemmie, you were the strong one," Melba says, slipping her arm around her sister.

"You came from a whole family and weren't crippled like I was. There was nothing for you to overcome. Me, I had to learn how to be strong. That's hard right now. I'm dealing with a crisis in my life and trying to redirect my career. So you're right; I'm feeling wounded. But there's no reason you can't be part of my reconstruction and I can also be a part of yours.

"This is the perfect time for us to help each other. We can do that. We're sisters."

On a bitter cold day in January, Whitney Williams celebrated her 11th birthday at a lively party held in an indoor amusement park near her home in suburban Chicago. Between coughing bouts that wracked her thin body, she and her girlfriends rode the ferris wheel and the roller coaster, shrieking as the rickety cars careened up and down the noisy little track. When it came time for her to blow out the candles and eat the cake, Whitney closed her eyes, clasped her hands, and asked God to find a cure for AIDS.

Whitney wasn't merely making a sensitive birthday wish. She was pleading for her life. There are approximately two thousand children in the United States suffering from AIDS, and Whitney is one of eighty-five particularly baffling cases: Doctors have no idea how she became infected with the AIDS virus. Her parents are both HIV-negative. She's never received a blood transfusion or been sexually abused.

When Whitney discusses her illness with adults, she speaks like a wise old woman. "I'm not afraid of dying," she says coolly and calmly. "It's stupid to be scared. I have strength inside my heart. I don't think God will take me this early."

But in an unguarded moment, lying in bed next to her seven-year-old sister Becky, she awakens from a bad dream and forgets to put on her mask of maturity. "Becky," she sobs. "I had this nightmare that I was dying. I was lying in my casket and Mommy was standing there crying because she couldn't help me."

Becky wipes her sister's tears. "That's why I like to sleep with you. So I can cuddle with you and protect you from nightmaries."

"It's nightmares, not nightmaries, and, to tell you the truth, cuddling doesn't help much with nightmares. You have to remember what I told you."

"You mean about guardian angels? You told me that when we sleep a guardian angel watches over us. And when you go to heaven, you'll be my guardian angel sister. Only when I wake up in the morning you won't go away. You'll stay with me all the time and you'll give me hugs. Only I won't be able to hug you back because my arms will go right through you."

Whitney and
Becky:
The Williams
Sisters

"One of the most interesting things about our careers is that neither one of us set out with any dreams of ever being ballerinas," says Deborah Hadley, principal dancer with the Seattle-based Pacific Northwest Ballet.

Tamara Hadley, her younger sister, a principal dancer with Philadelphia's Pennsylvania Ballet company, nods. "We danced because it was fun, but I tried to quit every summer. I hated getting sunburned and having to wear those scratchy leotards. Mommy would say, 'Just hang in there,' but I dreaded it. Then in winter it would be all right again. But, no, I never longed to be a ballerina. I liked my classes but I never liked the competition. Neither of us were ever bun heads. We didn't eat, drink, think ballet, and get like little toothpicks."

Like it or not, they would ultimately have to deal with competition. But while they could not control the rivalry among other dancers, they found a way to prevent it from destroying their own close relationship. Once they became professional ballerinas, "dancing together just wasn't ever discussed," Debbie says. "We always knew it was healthier for our careers to be totally separate."

The establishment of their careers was choreographed in a rocky point-counterpoint rhythm. Deborah hit stardom early when, at age 15, she was plucked out of her hometown San Diego company by the Jeoffrey Ballet in New York. A negative experience in the Big Apple soon soured her on the dance world, and she quit, got married, and had children. But she always remained peripherally involved in ballet, taking classes and appearing occasionally on the local stage.

Meanwhile, in high school, Tamara packed away her toe shoes to be a cheerleader and gymnast instead. Five years later when she returned to ballet, she had a very different attitude. "You can't do ballet half-assed," she says. "I buckled down, lost ten pounds, got serious, and realized I loved to dance." Now it was her turn for success. She was signed by the Pennsylvania Ballet and moved to Philadelphia, leaving her sister behind in San Diego.

Six years passed. Deborah, at what she calls the lowest point in her life, living on food stamps, coping with a failed marriage, and raising two children, came to visit Tammy in Philadelphia and was persuaded to take a company class. In no time she was hooked all over again. "It was like, oh my God, I can't believe how much I missed this. But who would hire a divorced 27-year-old with two kids who hasn't danced in five years?" How about a friend of her sister's who'd just started a new ballet company in Seattle? Debbie pawned her inheritance—her grandmother's ring—to pay for the airfare to attend an audition and was hired on the spot.

That is how these two sisters wound up dancing on opposite coasts. Ironically, they both perform in Balanchine-oriented companies with similar repertoires, where they typically dance the same roles.

"It's so great," says Tammy, "to pick up the phone, ask 'What are you doing this season?' and have this common ground of sympathy for the demands of the role. Oh, you've got to do that grueling variation. That's too bad. Or, oh you'll get to do blah, blah. That's fun. We give each other the inside scoop on choreographers, too. We have this base that we feel and work from, and it has nothing to do with how often we talk or see each other."

"It's fabulous to be able to have that really sympathetic ear where you know the other one really, really knows," says Debbie. "It's given us a mutual respect for what the other has done because we've both done it and know how hard it is."

Throughout their careers, the sisters have danced on the same program only once, at a festival, and that was by choice rather than by accident.

"It's not because we're competitive or jealous. We've never been," Tammy explains. "Mother did not pit us against each other. It was always praise, praise, praise. It's that the dance world is such a closed circle. So gossipy. If we danced together somebody would say, 'Her feet are better than yours.' Or 'She does this better than you.' Why set yourself up for that? We thought it would be smarter to be in very distant companies so that we wouldn't ever be compared to each other."

"People have tried all along the way to compare us," Debbie says, "and we just never buy into it. They want to see us perform together on the same stage, and we say, 'Are you kidding? Just forget it.' "

"Besides," says Tammy, "I think she's better than I am and she thinks I'm better than she is."

"Our relationship has never been in jeopardy," Debbie says. "We are as close as two people could be. No matter how far away we are, there is this base that we feel and work from. The only reason we've stayed separate is to protect our careers."

Pat and Gail:
The Henion Sisters

"I remember I'd come back early from a Saturday playtime and walked in on my parents making love," says writer Gail Sheehy, becoming for a moment a precocious eight-year-old with a wicked secret.

"It was quite shocking, and they had to immediately come up with some kind of cockamamie story as a cover. They said they were trying to make me the sister I wanted. That was great, because now they had to deliver the goods or I wouldn't have believed them. I giggled to myself all day long. This was really neat. They were finally going to do what I'd been asking them to do for years." Just about nine months later, Pat was born. "It was amazing," Gail says with a tender smile. "Here was this live baby. Someone to play with and love. Just a delightful addition."

The nine-year age gap between the two sisters eliminated the potential for competition, and also defined their roles in the family. Gail easily played the part of the older, wiser, grown-up. Trish, as Gail calls her, acted out the adorable child. But the beauty in their relationship for these sisters turned out to be its changing nature.

"Once you move out of the family household," Gail says, "you don't have to be the good-deed sister or the obedient sister any more. There's no specific role one must play with one's sister. With husbands you have a love contract and matters that need negotiating. With children you have all the complications that come with resenting advice and direction. But with your sister, there is no ulterior motive. Nothing done out of obligation. How you are depends on where you are and what you need from each other. For Trish and me, our adult phase started when we went to Paris together.

"I was 29, already slightly bruised, in turmoil from the end of my first marriage, and raising a daughter alone. Trish was 20, a kid kind of sprouting,

coming to visit me in New York for two weeks on her way to Boston. Then I got an assignment from *Cosmopolitan* to fly to Paris, go out with three sexy Frenchmen, and find out why they're the world's best dates. I arranged to get Trish ticketed as my researcher and took her along. It was a gas! I'd only been to Europe a couple of times; she'd never been outside the country. It was so delicious to show this to someone you love. We had a marvelous hotel and stayed in a room with big shutters that opened onto a courtyard. I still remember the sun streaming in every morning. It was this great new world and we were experiencing it together.

"Later, we went to Ireland and as we were driving along, one of us said, 'We're like those sisters who wrote *The Joy of Cooking!*' They were two women who'd never married, and they realized they were going to spend their lives together, but neither one knew how to cook. So they learned together and wrote this cookbook and just enjoyed life with each other. This will be Trish and me, I thought. We'll always play together, have adventures, find ways to have fun. I very clearly recognized that something new had happened, a whole new possibility in life. We didn't have to be big and little sister anymore. We could be friends. We could be pals."

Pat has been listening thoughtfully, and laughs softly. "Well, I was like the man who came to dinner. I still haven't left New York. That trip did set up the shape of our relationship. The second thing that molded it was taking care of Mom over a period of years when she was ill."

"That's one of life's tasks you don't learn in school," Gail says. "We did it well, really did it well. Somehow we learned to pass the baton between us."

"There was definitely a give-and-take," Pat says. "I might get a phone call, a distress signal, and I'd call Gail to tell her about it and what I was doing. She'd make suggestions, sometimes prop me up. Her efforts would keep me going."

"Once we went down and found Mom in a desolate state," Gail says. "All huddled up and turned in on herself. We began opening her up by massaging her, rubbing her feet, taking her into the shower, washing her hair, getting her into the sun. It was one of the most loving interactions I can ever remember because there weren't any words between us."

"Just physical things," Pat continues. "Later we'd say how happy we were to have each other there. Can you imagine going through this alone? We didn't have to elaborate. We both knew exactly what we meant. I think that experience took our relationship to another level. Made us more conscious that as we get older we might need that kind of care and one of us might be giving it to the other."

"We actually had some belly-splitting laughs outside that hospital room," Gail says. "It's so easy to be jovial around my sister because she knows how to make me laugh—and laugh at myself. She offers me laughter and forgetting. Takes me out of my head. That gives me the extra boost of energy to do the next mile and the next."

"When it comes down to who's going to empty Mom's bedpan, you have to have a sense of humor," Pat says. "Gail supports me, too. It's very important to both of us to keep things on an equal footing. She gives me intellectual stimulation. Sometimes financial help. She's encouraged me to go on with my education—I'm getting a Masters in English at Hunter College. Lately I've been concerned about what I call the wild-woman side of Gail, the part that loves physical challenges. She doesn't do enough of that because she spends so much time writing at the word processor. So I told her I'm taking over her physical activity, making arrangements to go kayaking and things like that. Maybe we'll do an Outward Bound together."

Pat and Gail's relationship works because they work hard at nurturing and protecting it. "Sometimes the boundaries are getting uncomfortable or we're falling into a funny pattern," Gail explains. "And even though we live close by, one of us will write a long letter and the other will always respond with a long answer. We get it all out before a misunderstanding creeps underneath, like a vine that's all twisted. We write each other thank-you notes, too.

"Ever since our trip to Paris, we haven't taken our relationship for granted. I always remember what I felt then. My marriage was ending and I said to myself, 'Husbands come and go; children come and eventually they go. Friends grow up and move away. But the one thing that's never lost is your sister.' "

Hope and Mary Binney: The Montgomery Sisters

"We are three years, one month, one week and two days apart, and Hope is older," Binney announces.

"That's why I'm so protective," Hope retorts. "I always used to beat up anybody who bothered her, and I still protect her. Two years ago Binney broke her hip in India—she was there taking pictures for her lectures—and I got her out by calling our dear friend, Walter Annenberg, in California.

"It was New Year's Eve and I told him, 'My sister is stuck at Heathrow Airport with a broken hip and no way to get out for four days.' Well, it was awfully lucky that Walter happened to be with Richard Nixon and the British Ambassador. They called British Airways and bumped four people because she had to be out flat. You see, we always help each other."

Binney nods in agreement. "She helped me, all right. She got Walter and made it happen. She has this will to get things done."

Hope and Mary Binney have been standing up for each other since they were little girls, even though they chose different paths. Hope became an athlete; Binney, an artist.

"I knew so little about fine art that I thought Goya was a gigolo I met in Paris," Hope says. "I can't tell you why we have this tight bond. Our lives today are totally different, except for how we give parties. Mother trained us how to set a table, to entertain, and be charming. But we never did anything together, so there was never any rivalry."

"I respect my sister very much because I feel she's honest," Binney offers.

"But dear, you're honest, too," Hope counters.

"I know that when Hopey was sent away to boarding school, I missed her terribly and thought it would be wonderful if I went, too. But mother said no."

"I wanted her to come. She was part of my life."

"We never had any secrets from each other. Hope told me never to keep secrets."

"I told her all the things I learned and I always had the greatest respect for my sister because she was so artistic," Hope says. "We had a dancing class in the house and Bin was the star. She moved beautifully. Even did toe dancing. I could never do that."

"Not so," Binney says. "You were very good."

"I was terrible. One time I did this Russian dance and I was stiff as a ramrod."

"It was Hungarian to the *Rhapsody* by Brahms, and no, you weren't."

"Do you remember when father leased that sailing boat and we spent the winter on the Nile?"

"You were 17 and I was 14 and we decided to fall in love with one of the sailors. Of course, we never spoke to them. We just spent our time waiting for them to climb the mast so we could look at them. I remember I'd just turned 14 and I was so excited, because I thought now everyone would come calling on me as they did on Hope. She said I shouldn't count on it, and she was right. Hope always had more

beaus than I did. The night she decided to marry Edgar she had five other proposals that very evening."

These memories are still vivid, part of the sisters' connection, forged long ago in the bedroom they shared from childhood to adolescence.

"We lived in a huge house, but mother put us together because it was more convenient," Hope recalls. "Every night we had this unbreakable ritual. We'd kneel down together and say our prayers. Then we'd kiss each other and get in bed. That was our time to talk. There was always so much to talk about. After we talked, we'd say this little rhyme we'd made up, alternating the parts until we got it all out. 'Good night . . . Sleep tight . . . No dreams . . . I hope you don't wake up . . . Stay tucked in bed . . . Go right to sleep . . . No more talking.' And we'd touch hands with each other. We never went to bed without touching hands."

These two girls, growing up like princesses on a 750-acre estate with thirteen servants, sharing a tutor, a governess, a playroom, and a bedroom followed very different paths. Hope became a nationally-known championship horsewoman, one of the first to ride in Madison Square Garden, and today manages a large working dairy farm. Her willful, madcap personality was the inspiration for the heroine in *The Philadelphia Story*, written by Phillip Barry, a family friend. "It was really about Hope's *attitude*, not her life," Binney says. "She's been married for sixty-eight years. And my sister is *much* prettier than Katharine Hepburn."

Hope graciously deflects the compliment. "I did want to do everything and know everybody. I loved people and parties." Indeed, she succeeded—from sharing deck chairs with Winston Churchill on the Onassis yacht to meeting every American president since Roosevelt.

Binney, by contrast, pursued a life in the arts. She was a fine enough pianist to play once with the Philadelphia Orchestra, but, put off by stage fright, she turned to dance, and founded and ran a ballet

company for ten years. She ultimately became a published photographer. And, in her own way, she, too, was an iconoclast. Tired of waiting for the man of her dreams, in 1940 she adopted two children.

"I was determined to have a family even if I didn't have a husband. Then, one night I went to a dinner party and there was a beautiful man sitting next to me. I played the piano after dinner as well as I could to attract his attention, and afterwards we danced on the carpet." Within four months, they were married. Eighteen years later he died, and she never remarried.

Two remarkable women. Two unusual and highly individual lives. Yet they've remained as close as they were seventy-some years ago when every night they reached out and touched hands before they closed their eyes.

"You see, it doesn't matter whether or not we had similar interests or lifestyles," Binney says. "We learned to love each other as children, and we never stopped."